In Season and Out, Homilies for Year B

In Season and Out, Homilies for Year B

William J Grimm

UCAN ·)))›

2015

ISBN
9781925371208   Bill Yr B   paperback
9781925371215   Bill Year B   hard back
9781925371222   Bill Year B   ebook
9781925371239   Bill Year B   pdf

Layout by UCAN and Astrid Sengkey
Cover design by Astrid Sengkey. Original artwork 'Having Enough, and Yet More'
by Soichi Watanabe is used with the permission of the artist.
© 2013. All rights reserved.
Text Minion Pro Size 10 &11

Published by:

An imprint of the ATF Ltd.
PO Box 504
Hindmarsh, SA 5007
ABN 90 116 359 963
www.atfpress.com
Making a lasting impact

Table of Contents

Lent

Easter Season

Foreword

The Catholic Church lives on two lungs—Word and Sacrament. They reach their clearest expression and celebration for the Church's life in the Eucharist—the "source and summit of the Church's life" as Vatican 2 puts it.

Father William J Grimm is a Maryknoll Missioner of 40 years experience in Asia—mostly Japan, but Hong Kong and Cambodia as well. In that time he has come to deepen his understanding of the distinctiveness of the message and person of Jesus Christ even in circumstances and among people that Jesus could never have known or imagined.

Every week for the Church's three year liturgical cycle, Fr. Grimm gives visitors to www.ucanews.com—UCAN—the benefit of his learning, prayer, wisdom and experience. Each week, his homilies for Sundays and special feasts are seen by some 3,000 visitors to the main UCAN site and with subtitles on UCAN's Vietnamese and Chinese sites.

We are delighted to offer the texts of these pastoral homilies.

Michael Kelly SJ
Publisher

www.ucanews.com

First Sunday of Advent (B)

Though Advent has four Sundays, we celebrate with three virtues three comings of Christ in three tenses. Three threes!

With Christmas decorations all over, it is easy to forget that Advent is a time of coming rather than a preparation for Christmas. The Gospel about the coming of the Lord when we least expect him makes it clear that we are not merely preparing for December 25.

That day, we celebrate the past tense coming of the Lord, the birth of Jesus. He was born like us, grew up like us, died like us. He had a mother, a father, relatives, teachers, friends and foes. He worked as a carpenter. He called followers, and directed them to a new way of life before God long ago and far away. And we believe in him.

Faith is our love of that man. We love him in the life he led, in the Scriptures that teach us of him, in the Church that guides us to him. We gather each week to remember him by breaking bread. We commit ourselves to saying that he was real, not a legend. He was someone we can love as we love other people we have known in the past, people no longer present.

But, there is a difference, because his coming in the past is not all. We also await his future coming. He "will come again in glory to judge the living and the dead."

I'm not sure I want to meet the One who knows all there is to know about me. At some time in the future, I will face the absolutely just judge who will know exactly what I deserve, and will render the fairest judgment on my life: "Guilty."

Yet, we wait in joyful hope for his coming. Do we look forward to being forced to see how sordid our lives have been? No. We look forward to the full verdict: "Guilty, but forgiven."

That is the source of our hope, love in the future tense. We love the Lord who will come bringing final forgiveness and final joy to our lives.

I fall into problems, though, if I concentrate solely upon the past and future comings of the Lord. Especially as Christmas approaches,

I get sentimental over Christmases past. Eventually, I forget the real man Jesus altogether.

If I focus upon his future coming as Judge and Savior, I get complacent. After all, we've already waited two millennia. In addition, the future is an abstraction. At least I've lived through the past and have some idea of what it was. The future may be daydreamed about, but my guesses are empty speculation. So, I don't bother; I sit back and forget.

That is why the most important coming of Christ is neither in the past nor the future. It is his coming today, in the present tense. He comes in my time, my life.

Ironically, this most important coming is often the hardest to recognize. His past coming is available to us in the Gospels. His future coming is not available to us, though when it comes, there will be no mistaking it.

His present coming is paradoxically present, yet hidden. It is too present, too quick, for us to devote time to recognizing it. He sneaks up on us, demanding instant recognition and instant response. And he does it in disguise. It takes a ready heart to see him. It takes the fullness of the love that shows itself as faith and hope, love in itself.

Jesus comes in someone needing help, the child lost in a crowd, the lonely neighbor, the family member across the table. He is the child who asks a wise question, the adult who gives a wise answer. He may be a poet, a politician, a pauper or a prince. Sometimes I even catch a glimpse of him in the mirror. He comes in so many disguises that I usually miss him.

When Jesus comes in the present, he looks for real, practical love. Not an emotion, but action. My faith means nothing if I can't see and love him today. My hope is wasted if I refuse his invitation to love him now. If I'm not willing to see the Lord today, I have reason to fear seeing him at the end.

Faith, hope and love are virtues directed toward past, future and present. In Advent, we remind ourselves to be ever ready to meet and love the Lord who has come, who will come, who comes.

Second Sunday of Advent (B)

In this Church year, we will reflect upon the Gospel of Mark, the first of our four gospels to be written, and the only one to call itself a Gospel. The word is actually two Old English words put together: *gōd* ("good") and *spel* ("news"). Good news. It is a translation of the Greek word that Mark uses in today's reading, *euangelion*.

"Here begins the gospel of Jesus Christ, the Son of God," is the way Mark opens, and this one sentence sums up his entire text. Right from the start, Mark declares that what he has to tell is good news.

Let's stop for a moment and think about that. Do I really think of my faith as good news? Sometimes, I suppose, I do. But I'm more inclined to think of it as ideas to which I give assent, moral rules which I obey (or disobey), a structured community living in history (including my history).

Does the world at large think of our faith as good news? If folks believed it to be good news, there would be more of them joining us. Perhaps they don't see it as good news for themselves because we don't show that it is good news for ourselves.

Why do you suppose that is? Is it possible that our faith in the Good News is so weak that we fear putting it up against the bad news? Are we afraid to match the gospel to the pain, confusion, doubt and evil we see around us and within us? Perhaps we fear that the gospel won't measure up, or even that it is irrelevant to what bothers the world. Do we fear that the bad news will smash our gospel faith, and so we keep it safe to be brought out only on Sundays and holidays?

Yet, for the Good News to be good, it must face what's bad. Most of us are experts at bad news. Being experts at bad news is, paradoxically, good. At least we know where the Gospel is needed in our lives, know the shape of the hole in our lives that the Good News must fill to really be good news.

The answer to it all is a relationship with Jesus Christ. And so Mark says, "the gospel of Jesus Christ." The bad news in my life has an answer in the One who went to the Cross. He knows the bad news, because, like us, he lived with it. He knew the confusion of childhood, the insecurity of adolescence, the betrayal of love, the fear and agony of death. He knew his own bad news, and he knows mine.

We are very busy people. Just getting to church on Sunday seems to be about as much as I can handle. Give time for prayer or quiet reflection? Give time to read Scripture and other faith-nourishing, faith-challenging things? Spend time and energy with and for my neighbor? I'd love to, but I'm just too busy. And yet, that is where I will develop the relationship with Christ that will be the Good News for my bad news.

Why is that? Mark also proclaims that in his first sentence. Jesus Christ is "the Son of God." In knowing Christ, I know the Son of God whose death on the cross became the source of life. God's love is stronger than the bad news. The resurrection of Christ is the guarantee of that strength. Our baptism into the death and resurrection of Christ is the guarantee that we share it.

That's good news for you, for me, for everyone. And good news is for sharing. Just as we recommend good restaurants and good films, once we know Christ as good news, we recommend him. How? By living lives that really look as if they are touched by good news.

Once I really know Christ as good news, others will want to know the secret of my joy in pain, my confidence in confusion, my hope in the face of death. The pain, the confusion, the death will not go away. They will be, however, the place where I meet Christ more deeply because I'm not afraid to bring my faith there. The pain, confusion and death will be the bad news where the Good News happens.

And so, in Advent we make a bit more effort to welcome the Lord into our lives and into our hearts, so that we can indeed know him as Son of God, as Good News.

Third Sunday of Advent (B)

A minister described his vocation in the words of John the Baptizer: "a voice in the desert, crying out: 'Prepare the way of the Lord!'"

That is a description not only of the Baptizer's vocation, or the minister's, but of the vocation of every Christian. We are all meant to be voices in the desert, calling upon the world to prepare the Lord's way.

TV nature shows teach us that the desert is full of life, color, beauty and documentary makers. But, for people who lived in the cities and towns of the Middle East two millennia ago the desert was home to scorpions, vultures, poisonous snakes and demons, a place of loneliness, barrenness and death.

That's the sort of place where John felt called to proclaim the coming of the Lord. Why? Well, it doesn't take much thought or experience to admit that loneliness, barrenness and death can be true, if partial, descriptions of the whole world. Especially when viewed without faith, the world looks like a desert. John was in a place that symbolized the world of those who heard him.

We, too, are sent into the desert to do what John did. Our sandy wastes may be paved and our vultures may carry cell phones, but where we live can be as much a desert as the area around the Jordan River.

We are in the desert, and like John we have a vocation here. We must issue a call to prepare the way of the Lord.

But, what is this way of the Lord? I think the English word "way" is an excellent starting point for reflecting upon what it is that we are called to do with our faith. Two of its many meanings will suffice.

The first meaning, the one Isaiah used, is a road from one place to another. A way has a starting point and a goal toward which one heads. To prepare the way is to make sure the road is ready for travel.

Ways are defined by where they go. Where are we headed? The object of our journey is the full, uninterrupted, unweakened and unending experience of the love of God. We have to name it, so we call it heaven. Jesus called it the Reign of God.

So, preparation of the Lord's way to which we call our fellow desert creatures is preparation to experience the love of God. Since we learn best by doing, we invite, challenge and offer opportunity to our fellows to love and be loved. That's where the way of the Lord moves into a second meaning of "way" — a style of doing or being.

The style of those journeying toward the Lord is characterized by certain ways of dealing with fellow travellers: love (of friends and foes alike), justice (in the Biblical sense of taking special care to look out for the weak) and peace (not the mere absence of conflict, but an environment in which all can live as children of God).

Since every human being is in the desert, since every human being is on the journey to the Lord, preparing the way is a vocation for all men and women, Christian or not.

This is the reason we, the Church, have something to say about the way the world runs. Society, politics, economics, religion, the arts, the sciences are all subject to encouragement or correction as they aid or hinder preparing the way of the Lord.

That's a big responsibility. It's so frightening that perhaps our greatest sins are due to our fear of what calling the world to prepare the way of the Lord might cost. After all, John the Baptizer lost his head. Jesus was killed on a cross. What will the neighbors think? I need a lot more courage. Where can I find it?

Courage comes from the conviction that I am not alone. We are a community of saints and sinners who call the world to journey toward the Lord, to live in the way of that journey. What is more, we journey with the risen Lord who called himself The Way.

The place we really live our faith is not in a church. It is in the desert of our workplaces, our schools, our streets, our homes. There is no other place for the world to hear our call to prepare the way of the Lord, to join us on the way of and to the Lord.

Fourth Sunday of Advent (B)

The angel appears to Mary and says, "Rejoice, O highly favored daughter! The Lord is with you. Blessed are you among women." But Mary is "deeply troubled by his words." Why would anyone be troubled to hear that God favors her?

Let's imagine the scene. Mary has been doing laundry, and is drying her hands on her apron while the messenger of God speaks to her. She is no one special, just one of the many women in Nazareth who expect to spend a lifetime bearing babies, baking bread, cleaning house and looking after their husbands. Though there have been great women in the history of Israel, they are long dead. Why should she expect anything special from God or anyone else? Yet, here is an angel telling her she is specially favored by God.

There is a problem in being specially favored by God. It usually means God has chosen one to do something special, given a call that requires a break from a comfortable everyday existence to do something that may make no sense.

Mary's society may not have offered her much of a life, but at least it was secure. It was the life her mother, her grandmother and all the women she knew had lived. There was security in it and even some personal fulfilment according to the terms she had been taught to seek. What if God's favor meant abandoning that security and being someone other than her society envisioned?

That's the trouble with God. Just when we think our lives are going smoothly — not great, but not bad — God shakes us up with a call. Frequently, it's less pleasant than we think the appearance of an angel might be. It may be something that can drive us to despair.

The difficulty is that we are willing to settle for less than what God offers. We are offered God, and want the world instead. Sometimes it takes wrenching separation to prepare us to accept God's offer.

And what of Mary? The angel offers her an unplanned pregnancy, the risk of a broken engagement, the likelihood of ostracism by family and friends. Had she answered, "Thanks, but no thanks," she would have been a very sensible woman. Yet, Mary was not sensible.

It takes people who are not sensible people obeying unsensible calls that are not sensible things in order to bring Christ to the world.

But, why Mary? There would have been a rabbi in town who had dedicated his life to the Law of God and service to God's people. Just about any man would have been better educated than Mary. There would have been more powerful people, more socially prestigious people. Even among the women in town, there would have been wives of prominent men, mothers of many sons. Why did God favor an unmarried girl?

God doesn't choose the way we would. God chooses worldly weakness to proclaim divine power. That's the reason Mary was chosen and the reason we have been chosen.

All of us know deep down that we're poor weak sinners, lost in the world and hoping that no one will notice we're not really grown-ups yet. And God has chosen us to be bearers of Christ for the world.

We share Mary's vocation. She was chosen to bear the Savior. In our Baptism, we have been appointed to do the same, to bring Christ to the world, to be Christ for the world. Mary gave Jesus a body, so do I, so do you.

The story of Mary is our story, too. Or, it can be. The key is in our response. The whole story of Christmas depended upon one woman's willingness to say, "I am the handmaid of the Lord. Let it be done to me as you say." Am I willing to say the same?

As we celebrate our final Sunday before Christmas, Mary's willingness to say "yes" is an example and a challenge to each of us. Am I as ready as she to say "Yes!" to God's call to bring Christ into the world? Am I as ready as she to risk what doing the will of God might mean in my day-to-day life? If I can follow Mary's example, then my life will be Christmas for my brothers and sisters, the coming in unlikely circumstances of the Savior of the world.

Holy Family (B)

Matthew and Luke (the only New Testament writers who present pictures — sometimes contradictory — of Jesus' infancy and childhood) did not intend to give a chronicle of the early life of Jesus.

They wrote introductions to their accounts of the life, death and resurrection of the man Jesus. So, they left out details of his teething, first steps, toilet training, weaning, puberty and all the other events of his early life that we must assume occurred. Their infancy and childhood narratives are meant to tell us about the adult, and only about him.

So, then, what does the story of Jesus in the temple tell us about the vocation of Jesus?

Throughout his Gospel and the Acts of the Apostles, Luke lays stress upon the Jerusalem temple. It is Luke who tells of Jesus saying to his parents that the temple is his father's house. Luke shows us the infant Jesus being carried into the temple, not a usual practice in those days when Jews were scattered all over Israel and the rest of the world. The message is that Jesus is the One who from the moment of his coming really belongs in the temple because he is the real divine presence among the People of God.

When "guided by the Spirit, Simeon came into the temple," he was seeking the Lord. When he found him, he said a prayer that proclaims Jesus as the fulfilment of all the hopes of those who rely upon God's promise. Not only that, Simeon also praises God because Jesus is the fulfilment of the unspoken hopes and dreams of those who do not even know God. "My eyes have seen your salvation which you have prepared in the presence of all peoples."

Then Simeon tells Mary that Jesus is a sign that is opposed, and that she herself will be pierced with a sword. Traditionally, this is taken to refer to her pain at the crucifixion. However, it has a broader meaning, one that includes all of us. We believers, like Mary, are faced over and over again with Jesus forcing us to make a decision to follow him, a decision that can be heart-rending because it is ultimately an embrace of the cross.

Then comes Anna. Luke does not put any words into her mouth, but in a sense, she is a more important speaker than Simeon. He talks to Mary and Joseph. Anna spoke "about the child to all who were looking for the redemption of Jerusalem." In other words, Anna is a model of the Church, the community that speaks of Jesus to all who are looking for redemption.

We are all seekers. Some of us may say we are looking for God. More of us, probably, put it in different terms. We are looking for love, for happiness, for peace, for some sort of answer to a deep-down unease we feel but cannot put into words. This searching is one of the things that appears to distinguish us from other animals.

In our seeking, we sometimes settle for answers that eventually show themselves to be no answers at all. Sadly, many of us then decide there either is no answer or that the very quest is a neurosis rather than one of the God-given glories of humanity.

If there were no answer to our search and longing, then, indeed, our lives would be futile. What use is there for a hunger that cannot be filled? What sense can there be to an existence defined in part by something that is meaningless?

But, there is an answer. That is what the temple was all about. It was a proclamation in stone that God was present among the people and that their search leads to a real place. That real place is not merely a building; it is the presence of God.

That presence is not limited to a particular building or location or people or even a religion. It is a person who can come to us and be with us anywhere, any time. It is Jesus in what he said, what he did, what he was and what he is.

So, Simeon and Anna went to the temple and met the Lord, the answer to their search and ours that God has "prepared in the presence of all peoples," including us.

Epiphany (B)

The schoolboy sitting in front of me on the bus was carrying a textbook titled *Advanced Physics for Hong Kong*. I presume the title of the book referred not to some supposed uniqueness of physical laws in Hong Kong, but to the fact that the text was written for students whose first language is not English, or that it used examples familiar to people in Hong Kong. In other words, there was probably a perfectly logical explanation for the title.

However, that title started me thinking about the ways we sometimes think that a particular place, race, nationality or whatever is somehow special. In fact, everyone is special, since every single person is a child of God, made in the image of God and given a special vocation that no other living being will ever share.

Epiphany is the feast on which we celebrate the fact that all people are sons and daughters of God. The wise men who pay homage to Jesus stand for all the people of the world. That is symbolized in the custom of representing them as members of different races.

Throughout history, we humans have been exclusionists. Sometimes we have gone beyond exclusion to outright persecution. For some reason or other, or no reason at all, we view people who differ from us as remote from us. The less we know about them, the more we believe stereotypes and fictions, and then act upon those misconceptions.

Today, the Church says that Christians cannot follow the way of the world in this matter. Today we see that God's offer of salvation in Christ, God's love, is not limited by colored shapes on a map. Anyone and everyone is welcome.

It need not have been that way. After all, Jesus is the Messiah promised to Israel. He came to a particular people in a particular time. He may not have been what they were expecting, but he was certainly theirs. All of theology could have been taught from a book titled *Advanced Salvation for the Jews*, and the rest of us would have had no right to complain.

But, God issued an invitation to the whole world to join the new People of God. That is what today's Gospel story tells us. Easterners, that is, strangers and pagans, came to worship. Not only did they come, but they were led by a star of God. God not only welcomed them, God wanted them there.

It's unfortunate that we have settled on three as the number of those who came. The Gospel does not give any number. I think that we should represent today's feast with a long procession of people stretching beyond our sight and time. It should include all the wise men and women whom God has called to see the divine glory present among us in a man born some two thousand years ago to a Jewish mother. In other words, everybody.

So, should we go running out to buy more statuettes for our Christmas creches? Should we add airplanes and autos to the camels, and men and women of all ages and places to our three kings? Perhaps we should, since what we see influences what and how we believe. But, we are called to more by today's feast.

We are called to be Stars of Bethlehem, leading men and women to Christ. The chief vocation of the Church is to proclaim the Good News to all nations. How do I share in that great vocation?

All of us are called to be missionary in our day-to-day lives. Our neighbors should be able to see the light of Christ shining in our words and deeds. Is my life such as to attract others to journey to meet the Lord?

I hope that at least on occasion, it is. But, I have to admit that there is much in me and in my life that would not draw others to look to Christ whose name I claim when I call myself "Christian."

Today, I am especially called to root out from my speech, my thoughts and my deeds all prejudice toward other races, religions, cultures, and so forth. I am called to be as welcoming in my life as God, who welcomed strangers to share the wonder of knowing Jesus. God, who sent a star once upon a time and sends us today to lead others to worship him. I could call it *Advanced Christianity for All the World*.

Baptism of the Lord
First Sunday of the Year (B)

"She's more Christian than most Christians."

Have you ever made a similar comment? The implication is that being Christian means being gentle, generous and gallant. Since gentleness, generosity and gallantry are not monopolies of the baptized, just about anyone can be called "Christian."

The feast of the Baptism of the Lord, provides an opportunity to reflect upon what my own baptism means, what it means to say, "I am a Christian." Obviously, I could not be claiming to be notably generous, gentle or gallant.

Could it be that there are two kinds of Christianity — the nice kind practiced by the unbaptized and the mediocre kind preached by the baptized?

According to the Acts of the Apostles, followers of Jesus were first called "Christians" in Antioch. The word means "partisans of Christ." It has nothing to do with the way people act, but refers to whom they follow.

In other words, a Christian is not defined as a nice person. To be a Christian is to have a relationship with Christ, to be one of his partisans.

So, we are wrong to say of someone who is not baptized that he or she is very Christian. He or she is very good. Virtue is not a Christian monopoly. It's a form of spiritual imperialism to call them Christian. They are good (by the grace of God that comes through Christ) on their own terms, not ours.

However, the problem is greater than calling Buddhists, Hindus, Jews, Muslims or even atheists Christian. The real problem is a poor understanding of Christianity that allows us to make the mistake in the first place.

Perhaps the greatest internal threat to the Church comes not from theological disputes, nor sectarian divisions. The danger is an attitude called "moralism," the belief that the Christian life consists in living a special way, acting in a particular way, doing certain things and refraining from others. It puts the focus on me rather than on God.

Basic Christianity is found in this week's Gospel: "You are my beloved Son. On you my favor rests." God chooses to make us sons and daughters. In baptism, we are united with Christ, the Son, and enter into a special way of meeting God, a way chosen by God, not us.

Our duty, then, as Christians is to grow in that relationship. Good deeds, a good demeanor and good intentions are not enough. In prayer, reflection, study and action we must deepen our relationship with God.

If we do that, then we will, in fact, act in a particular way toward others. As we grow more aware of and awed by God's parental love, we can only respond by showing that love to others. Might that be the reason that after hearing the Father's voice, Jesus embarks on his mission?

God has said to each of us at our baptism, "You are my beloved child. On you my favor rests." What am I going to do about it?

First, of course, I give thanks. Then, I give witness. I try to live a life that proclaims to the world that God loves us. I may be a very pleasant person while doing it. I may be an ogre. My personality may repel certain people, and even me. That does not matter.

What matters is that God loves me even in my unlikeableness. Life would probably be nicer for my fellows if I were as gentle, generous and gallant as many who are not partisans of Christ. But, it is the partisanship, not the personality, that makes a Christian.

Second Sunday of the Year (B)

Once upon a time, a young man visited a rabbi.

"Rabbi," said the youth, "I do not believe. Convince me."

The rabbi said, "Go, and for one year act like a believer."

The youth left, thinking, "I came looking for wisdom, and he tells me to play act!"

However, since the rabbi's advice would not be difficult to follow, he decided to give it a try. A year later, he returned and said, "Rabbi, I believe."

Today's Gospel passage contains the first words of Jesus in John's Gospel: "What are you looking for?" He addresses disciples of John who like the young man in the story, are seekers.

However, when Jesus asks what they are looking for, they can't come up with any answer except to ask where he is staying. Are they too shy to ask what this "Lamb of God" business means? Or, could it be that they do not know what they are looking for?

Jesus answers, "Come and see." He does not offer explanations. He merely tells them to join him. If they go with him, they will find what they are looking for. By the end of the day, Andrew proclaims, "We have found the Messiah!"

I often feel something is missing in my life, that there must be more to it than counting the days and years till I die. Something's missing, but I can't even say for sure what it might be. If the Lord were to ask, "What are you looking for?" I, too, might answer, "Uh, where are you staying?"

The "Come and see" of Jesus was not an invitation to see where he was staying. It was an invitation to come and find what they really were seeking.

The paradox of faith is that we only learn what we seek in life and from life as we find it. I know I want something; I don't know what I want; I'll know it when I get it.

The disciples had no idea what was in store for them. They could not have conceived of the cross, the resurrection, their own mission to the world, martyrdom, eternal life.

Like the young man, the disciples became believers through acting like believers. They followed Christ to where he lived near Bethany and where he lives in glory. Now they know where he stays.

I, too, approach Jesus looking for something. If someone were to ask what I'm after, I could only give partial answers, because I do not yet know the full answer I will receive through a lifetime, an eternity, of following the Lord.

So, Jesus says to me, "Come and see. Come and see where I am to be found today. Come and see what it is you are really looking for. Come and see the fullness of life to which I will lead you.."

How do I go? It's not a matter of waiting on a street corner for some prophet to point out Jesus walking by.

The Church, the community born when Andrew and his friend decided to follow Jesus, serves the function of the Baptizer, pointing to the presence of Jesus. So, one way to go after him is to be part of this community.

That means more than spending an hour a week at some ritual. This community is one of worship and service. We worship individually and communally. In addition, we serve our neighbor as Jesus did. When the disciples went with Jesus, they entered into a path of healing, forgiveness, and liberation for others. Such lives will lead us to what it is, whom it is, we are seeking.

"What are you looking for?"

"I don't know, Lord; show it to me."

"Come and see."

Third Sunday of the Year (B)

Long ago, on the way home from school, I saw an elderly woman with two shopping bags stopping to rest every few steps. I offered to help her.

"How far are you going?" I asked.

"Not far — just down the street."

We walked a few blocks. My arms were tired, but I was too proud to rest. Every so often, I asked if we were getting closer. Each time, she answered, "Not much farther — just down the street."

Finally, she turned into a side street.

"Is this the block?"

"Not far — just down the street."

We plodded a few more blocks. My fingers were aching and numb at the same time. Finally she led me into an apartment building.

"What floor are we going to?"

"Not far — just upstairs."

At each floor, I asked if this was the one she lived on. By the time we reached her fifth-floor apartment, I had been "not far"-ed into exhaustion.

Jesus in today's Gospel seems to have something in common with that woman. "The reign of God is at hand!" Well, he said that 2,000 years ago, and it still seems to be a long way off.

Something else Jesus says complicates matters. "This is the time of fulfilment." Is he referring to his own time, or to any time we hear his words? Why say this is the time of fulfilment, and then that it's still on its way?

So, where is it? If it's already here, we should be able to recognize it. Well, the reason we can't recognize it leads to the third thing Jesus says: "Reform your lives and believe in the good news!" The reason we don't see the reign of God is that our lives need reforming.

The reign of God is the fullness of God's presence with us, resulting in the forgiveness of sins, the establishment of just relationships among peoples, the sanctification of all creation as an offering to our Creator.

Can we see signs of that?

The clearest presence of the reign is Jesus, God's reign made flesh. "The time of fulfilment has come" is another way of saying, "Here I am!"

But are we too late? Have we missed the chance to experience the reign of God? Must we wait till the end of time?

No, because God's reign present in Jesus is carried on through the Church, sinful, weak and divided though it be. In the community of men and women struggling to be faithful to Christ, sharing God's love with friend, foe and stranger, there is the reign of God, even if not in its fullness.

And the reign of God is not confined to the Church. There are signs of that reign throughout the world.

The breaking of shackles that bind the bodies, minds and spirits of men and women, the advance of knowledge, the work of artists and the growth of solidarity among nations, cultures and religions of the world are all signs that God's reign is here, that the world is growing toward the vocation God has set for it.

The symbol of all this, our truest experience of God's reign, is the Eucharist. When we share the body of Christ, we are in the reign of God, united with all Christ's people in all times and climes.

I often miss that, which is why Jesus calls me to reform my life, to make it a sign of God's reign. Living a reformed life will clear my eyes, heart and soul to see God's reign in the Eucharist and in all it stands for — Jesus, the Church, the world.

This is the time of fulfilment. The reign of God is at hand. Let us reform our lives so that we may see it present and coming.

Fourth Sunday of the Year (B)

Interesting, isn't it, that an unclean spirit recognizes the Lord, but people cannot. In fact, the unclean spirit is the first one in Mark's gospel to proclaim Jesus as "The Holy One of God."

The people marvelled at Jesus' words, liking what and how he taught. They focused on his message. It's easy to imagine them discussing his teachings for days. In fact, some folks have been discussing them for two thousand years. The unclean spirit, on the other hand, does not talk about the message of Jesus, but about Jesus himself, who he is.

Scientists speak of "anti-matter," the absolute opposite to matter. Contact between matter and anti-matter results in the annihilation of both.

The unclean spirit knew that in the presence of Jesus it was faced with its opposite. So, it shrieked, "Have you come to destroy us?" The spirit knew who Jesus is because in Jesus it saw not teachings, but absolute good. The spirit saw the presence of God.

Eventually, people recognized who Jesus is. Christians know that he is, indeed, what the unclean spirit proclaimed him to be, "The Holy One of God." We follow the unclean spirit in proclaiming God's presence among us in Jesus Christ.

It is not hard to think that I have more in common with an unclean spirit than that. There is much in my life that is as anti-matter compared to the reality that is Jesus.

When I look beyond myself to the Church, I nearly despair. Our track record is not good at all. The terrible weapons that plague our lives were developed in the part of the world with the longest, most intense Christian influence.

Some of the world's worst persecutions have been perpetrated by Christians who tortured one another in inquisitions, and went after non-Christians in crusades, forced conversions and the Holocaust.

The destruction of the environment God created as a home for all, the creation of economic, social and political systems that deprive men and women of their dignity as children of God — all these can be laid before followers of Christ with the words, "Here are your real children."

Is this cause to give up, to decide that since we have so much of the demon about us we should not presume to proclaim Christ? Should we give up doing what the unclean spirit did?

The rest of the world is no less soiled and sordid than we. In fact, we can stand as a symbol of the world, know Christ on behalf of the world, and proclaim him for the sake of the world precisely because we are tainted with evil.

It is when I recognize how far I am from the goodness of God that I can understand the awesomeness of God's love. When we confess our sinfulness, we can see its opposite, the Holy One of God.

The first step in repentance is to admit our guilt, as when we go to confession. We admit our faults and failures out loud, making them painfully and embarrassingly real to ourselves. Then, we are presented with the sin-overpowering love of God when we most recognize our need of it.

And we come to a key difference between ourselves and the unclean spirit. The demon feared; we rejoice because we know that Christ, the Holy One of God, is only our opposite in terms of evil. In terms of love, we are beloved children of God.

Therefore we proclaim that the Holy One of God is among us, that there is hope for us in our uncleanness. We proclaim, like the spirit in the gospel, that Jesus is the opposite of our sinfulness.

It might even be proper to say a grateful prayer for that spirit, that it, too, might know Christ not as its enemy, but as the love of God offered to all us unclean ones. Perhaps in God's mercy, we and that spirit will one day share the joy of heaven.

Fifth Sunday of the Year (B)

Jesus had a problem finding time to pray. Whenever he tried to get away for some prayer, folks in need tracked him down. "Rising early the next morning, he went off to a lonely place in the desert; there he was absorbed in prayer. Simon and his companions managed to track him down; and when they found him, they told him, 'Everybody is looking for you!'"

That problem is not limited to Jesus. We all live with the fact that as we grow in love of God, there seems to be no time to pray, to meditate, to contemplate. Studies must be done, jobs must be performed, families must be raised. Whenever a free moment appears, someone or something seems waiting to steal it.

So, we feel guilty that we do not give God the time we think we are supposed to. But perhaps it is a mistake to make too great a separation between prayer and our everyday lives. Over the centuries, we have allowed a special vocation in the Church, monasticism, to become a sort of norm for what our religious life should be. We feel guilty when we do not (even though we cannot) give ourselves over to hours of daily prayer.

But most of us do not live in monasteries where the day is built around our prayer schedule. Most of us live in situations where the day is built around nothing in particular, unless chaos be something in particular. Our days are devoted to reaching the end of them with a modicum of dignity, energy, health, sanity and holiness.

We must look to someplace other than the monastery for a model, and we can find one in Simon Peter's mother-in-law. When we first hear of her, she is in bed with a fever. We all know that experience. Had she been a younger woman with little children running around, she might not have been able to take to her bed. She would still have been taking care of the kids who probably brought the fever home with them in the first place.

Jesus came to her, took her by the hand, and helped her up. Immediately, the fever went away. How did she respond to this healing? Did she glorify God? Did she thank Jesus? Did she tell the neighbors? Did she congratulate her son-in-law on his choice of friends? No, "she immediately began to wait on them."

In other words, her immediate response to the healing love of God in Christ was to get back to her everyday activity. She began to look after her guests, setting a table, making a meal, seeing to their comfort. The sorts of things we all, in varying ways, do all the time. Normal stuff.

The mystery of the Incarnation, the presence of God among us as one of us, means that the place to find God, the place to meet the Lord, is not on some special sacred mountain, nor in a desert cave. It is not in the forest nor in a cathedral. The place to meet the Lord is in my daily life, in normal stuff.

Therefore, it is a mistake to think that we must be engaged in prayer if we are to meet the Lord. We can meet him and serve him at every moment of our lives. Peter's mother-in-law knew this. When she encountered the saving power of God in Christ, she did the right thing. She got on with her everyday life.

Does that mean we need not pray? No. Prayer is a special time to experience our relationship with God in a less ambiguous way than we might while sitting at a keyboard, wiping runny noses (our own or others') or waiting for a traffic light to change.

Because it lacks the ambiguity of such times, my prayer time is, indeed, precious, and a hunger for it is natural. We want to spend time with the One who loves us best. However, Jesus' own experience teaches us that we must be willing to sacrifice our prayer time for the sake of others. Like Jesus, we must be ready and willing to leave our prayer for those who seek us out. Like Peter's mother-in-law, our encounter with God must get us back to normal stuff.

Sixth Sunday of the Year (B)

I told a well-educated, open-minded couple about a heartwarming encounter I had recently had with a boy whose body was badly deformed. The woman's face showed shock and disgust. Her education and values could not overcome some sort of inborn taboo against contact with someone who seems to be "unclean" in some way or other.

In our more honest moments, we can each find the same sense of taboo in ourselves. It may be directed toward those who look different, those who "have something wrong" with them, those of a different nationality, class, religion, sexual orientation or race, or any of a number of other things. Death is a sure case of it; our reluctance to touch corpses is not rational.

I am not immune to feelings that "something" about another might be somehow contagious or contaminating, and I have never met anyone totally free of such feelings. The particular thing by which we are repelled may vary from person to person and culture to culture, but the repulsion seems to be universal.

So, the restrictions that the Law of Moses put on lepers were not unusual. Even the leper crying out, "Unclean, unclean!" felt repelled by his or her own self.

Since such feelings are natural, perhaps we should just accept them, live with them, and try to disguise them when expressing them might be impolitic or impolite.

But, we Christians believe in something beyond the natural, the supernatural. Just what does that mean?

Movie makers have one definition of the supernatural. It's usually darkly threatening, especially to attractive women. Some shops have another definition involving crystals, mythological beasts, candles, aromas and angel lapel pins. Religious goods stores sell statues, books, posters and soupy music that purport to show the supernatural — usually as an other-worldly realm notable for its sentimentality and poor taste. What definition best expresses the reality of the supernatural?

None of the above is even close.

If you seek the supernatural, you will waste your time searching in movie theaters, shopping centers and church gift shops. You will even waste your time if you search for it by shutting yourself away from the world in order to pray and meditate.

The supernatural is not some realm apart from the world in which we live. Super-nature happens here, in nature, just as the comic-book character Superman lives in Metropolis with other men. The mystery of the Incarnation is that the realm of the supernatural is this world. If you want to see the supernatural, there is only one certain model — Jesus, and especially Jesus as we see him in today's Gospel.

What does he do that makes this passage such a clear picture of the supernatural? Is it the healing of the leper? No. Is it his telling the man to go to the priest to fulfill the religious code by making a sacrificial offering? No. The lesson in the supernatural comes in the words, "Jesus stretched out his hand and touched him."

As a man of his time and place and religion, Jesus would have been repelled by the sight of a leper. It was natural. Yet, Jesus overcame what was natural. He went beyond it to what was super-natural, literally "above nature" or "beyond nature." He touched a leper.

That touching healed the man. When Jesus went beyond what was natural, a miracle happened. The leper could be restored to membership in the community, to self-respect and to cleanness. His restoration was the result of a supernatural action, a touch.

We followers of Jesus are called to be supernatural. In other words, we must be people noteworthy for our willingness to go beyond the natural in us. That means developing the ability to look upon others as the sons and daughters of God, our brothers and sisters.

When we do that, we can transcend the "given," the natural, to get more deeply involved in the world — healing, teaching, forgiving, loving — being super-natural.

That is not easy. We must combat some of our deepest instincts in order to overcome our "taboo reflex." It is a battle we cannot hope to win without God's assistance, so when we succeed, we are signs of the supernatural power of God.

It is essential to the world that we succeed. In a world torn by our reluctance to see each other as beloved children of God, our only hope is in the supernatural. Continuing to live naturally will destroy any possibility of truly human life, and maybe even of any kind of human life.

Seventh Sunday of the Year (B)

People who have taken St. Augustine's words, "Outside the Church there is no salvation," at face value have done marvellous work to spread the Gospel. They have suffered pain, ridicule and martyrdom in order to save as many as possible who would be damned without the Church.

Sometimes they even forced people into the Church. Many of us are Christians because some ancestor was given the choice between baptism and death. Methods that we cannot approve bore blessings for us.

Were Augustine and so many others right? Is the Church essential to God's saving love for the world?

The story of the paralyzed man is about salvation. Jesus gives him spiritual healing, the forgiveness of sins. Jesus later gives the man physical healing as a sign that the forgiveness was real.

On what condition was the paralyzed man given salvation? Did he express faith in Jesus? Did he join the community of disciples? Did he ask for forgiveness or healing?

No, the man did and said nothing. We don't even know if he said "Thank you."

So, why was he forgiven?

The man was forgiven and healed because he had believing friends who carried him to Jesus. When they could not get into the house, they went up on the flat roof and tore part of it away. (Roofs were made of sticks covered with straw and mud, so it was not difficult to break through or to repair them later.)

Once the four had opened a hole in the roof, they lowered their friend to Jesus. The man was probably terrified that he might fall. He may have tried to stop them from doing something so potentially dangerous. Faith in Jesus was probably the farthest thing from the man's mind.

But it was not the man's faith that moved Jesus. It was the faith of his friends. "When Jesus saw their faith, he said to the paralytic, 'Son, your sins are forgiven.'"

The situation is similar to the case of the baptism of an infant who makes no declaration of faith. The child is baptized into the faith of the Church, present in the parents, godparents, the gathered community and the entire communion of believers in all times and climes.

So, the paralyzed man, like the baptized infant, is offered salvation because of the faith of others. Apparently, God's action on our behalf does not depend directly upon our faith — a comforting thought, since I probably most need that forgiving love at times when I am least faithful and least faith-filled.

What does that tell us about the Church? Might our vocation be that of the friends in the Gospel, believing, praying, worshipping and serving on behalf of the world?

The Incarnation teaches us that God acts through creation. We celebrate this every time we take bread and wine and share them as the sacrament of the Lord's presence among us. We speak of the Church as "the sign and sacrament of salvation," a community that makes God's saving action really present.

Perhaps God has made the faith and prayers of the Church the necessary instrument of salvation for the whole world. In that case, Augustine was right, but in a way he might not have realized. It may be that there is no salvation without the Church, but one need not be inside the Church to be saved.

If that be so, then what of the Church's vocation to mission? Is it sufficient to say our prayers for the rest of the world and otherwise leave it alone? We must look again at the friends of the paralyzed man.

They did not merely send a message to Jesus asking him to do something about their sick friend. They did what was practically necessary to ease the burden of the sick man.

We must do likewise for our sick world. There are two reasons for this. The first is that God works through our practical actions to bring healing, hope and wisdom. The second is that people have the right to see God's saving power at work. Jesus gave the man physical healing because he and those around him needed to be shown that God's forgiving love is real.

If through our service and witness our brothers and sisters can walk through the world with more hope, even if it means walking away from us, we must give thanks. If some of them decide to join us, then we rejoice, since the world will have yet others to be the Church without which the world is paralyzed, awaiting salvation.

Eighth Sunday of the Year (B)

It was common practice among Jews in the time of Jesus to fast. So, when the followers of Jesus did not follow this normal practice, people came to him to ask about it because a rabbi was responsible for his disciples' actions. If they did something that varied from common religious practice it would only be at the instigation of their master.

So, why didn't the companions of Jesus fast? His followers today do so in Lent and at other times. Why not then?

In his answer, Jesus refers to a wedding celebration, a time for food, drink, music, dance and fun. Fasting would be not only foolish, but bad manners as well. It would be a refusal to accept the gift of joy being offered to all who are present.

Jesus is saying, then, that his presence with the disciples is such a source of joy that fasting is out of the question. They should rather be eating, drinking, singing, dancing and laughing.

So, shouldn't our lives be full of eating, drinking, singing, dancing and laughing with never a practice so unjoyful as fasting? After all, doesn't the Church claim that Christ is still present with us today? Isn't the community of believers called the Body of Christ? Don't we speak of a real presence of Christ in the Eucharist?

Yes, Christ is still with us, but it takes faith to realize that. His presence among those disciples in Galilee was obvious. We have to make an effort to recall Christ's presence among us. It is not always easy. Instead of Jesus in front of me, I see other people, I see my work, I see myself with my weakness and failures. I get distracted.

I need training in order to recognize Christ. I must make an effort to force my meandering mind to turn to him. If I do so, then I am ready for joyful eating, drinking, singing, dancing and laughing.

A friend and I once visited a priest who lived in a remote place. Neither of us had ever met him before, nor had we ever been to his town. Our journey was long, hard and tiring. When we reached our destination hours late, our host opened his door to us and without preliminary words of greeting threw his arms out in a gesture of welcome and said, "First you wash. Then you eat. Then we talk!" He realized that the joyful visit required preparation. So, we washed away the dust of the journey, took care of our bodily needs and then had a wonderful time.

Perhaps that is the reason we followers of Jesus engage in ascetic activities from time to time. It is a way to withdraw from the distractions of our lives in order to celebrate the presence of Christ. It is a sort of cleansing of our minds and hearts from all that would distract us from recognizing Christ among us.

The objective of our fasting, then, is not to punish us. The objective is to know Christ's presence so fully that we become like his first disciples, like guests at a wedding. We fast in order to feast.

But, do we actually fast? Voluntary asceticism seems to have disappeared from the lives of many Christians. We live in a time when any sort of deprivation, whether voluntary or enforced, is considered evil. We do not like to do without.

However, our refusal to deprive ourselves occasionally for the sake of concentrating on knowing the Lord may deprive us of the opportunity to share the wild joy of the earliest disciples for whom being a follower of Jesus was as joyful as a party.

So, might this be the week that I give fasting a try, giving up a meal or a favorite television program or something else if only out of curiosity to see if that will help me know the Lord better, well enough to then eat, drink, sing, dance and laugh in joy at knowing him?

Ninth Sunday of the Year (B)

Did Jesus oppose the Sabbath? No, he opposed the fact that some people had made what was intended to be a day of rest into a heavier burden than work itself.

What does it mean to rest from labor? Does it mean to do nothing but go to church, to pray, to read Scripture? That does not sound very restful to me. Or, at least, it is not all that rest should be. Rest means relaxation, a loosening of the restraints of our day-to-day lives. It means, in one word, freedom. The Sabbath is freedom day.

But, freedom from what, freedom for what? What is my normal day like? It is largely a day controlled by others. Other people tell me the work I must do. Other people set my schedule. Other people determine when I rise, when I move, where I go, when I eat, when I have some time of my own. Those are the days when it seems I have been made for others' plans, programs and policies.

In the center of New York City's Manhattan Island, arguably the most driven city on the planet, is a park named unimaginatively but aptly Central Park. Surrounded by skyscrapers, it is a wildlife refuge as well as a people refuge. People leave the busy skyscrapers to stroll along the lakes, nap on the lawns, read on the benches, sketch the birds and trees and watch people watching people. Children go to climb on the statues or view the zoo. It is a geographic Sabbath. It may also be a model for what the Sabbath is meant to be. No one is forced to go to the park. No one is told what to do there. It is a place apart from the hustle and bustle.

A place apart, a time apart. That is the Sabbath. It is a day when we can cast aside our driven selves to be what we cannot be the rest of the week — creative, playful, relaxed. It is a day to be more a child of God than a child of the world. It is the most important day of the week. In that, the Pharisees were right. It is a day that should be treated as something really special.

The Sabbath is for us, and therefore is a day for us to grow in new ways. It is not a "do nothing" day, as if God created us to sit in front of

30

a TV to watch other people enjoy themselves at play. It is a day to try new recipes, to write a poem, to paint a picture, to make something with my own hands and skills, to explore a new neighborhood, to spend time with friends and family. It is a day to exercise the talents the Lord has given me that my day-to-day life stifles or hides. For the laborer, it is a day to rest weary muscles; for the desk worker, it is a day to exercise those muscles. So, the laborer reads a book while his neighbor digs a garden. It is a day to do nothing more "economically productive" than plucking the tops off of plants as we walk by.

Perhaps that is the reason Jesus adds a phrase that at first glance is confusing: "so the Son of Man is lord even of the Sabbath." Because the Sabbath is for us, Jesus is lord of it? It is justification for his allowing his disciples to be easy-going on the Sabbath, but it is more.

The Sabbath is the day when I have an opportunity (not always taken) to be a true companion of God. That does mean taking time to pray and celebrate our faith with my fellow disciples. But it also means doing much more. When I do so, when I take the time to be truly my own, truly God's, then the Son of Man is indeed the lord of the Sabbath, the day made for us.

Tenth Sunday of the Year (B)

I once had a "discussion" with a parish music minister about the hymn *Amazing Grace*. The choir was singing an "updated" version that changed the line praising God's grace for saving "a wretch like me." They sang, "Amazing grace! How sweet the sound that saved *and strengthened me!*"

The musician preferred the new version because it let us avoid having to look negatively at ourselves. I maintained that throughout my life I have done some things that have made me feel pretty wretched and find comfort in the thought that, even so, God's grace is available to save me.

The word "wretch" comes from an Old English word meaning "outcast" and has two meanings. One meaning describes someone who is despised by others, often with good reason. The second meaning refers to someone who is miserable, as an outcast would be.

The hymn was written by a man who deserved to be despised by others, and who through the amazing grace of God was rescued from his misery. John Newton was a slaver. He made his living transporting kidnaped men, women and children from West Africa in floating hellholes to the Western Hemisphere, where the survivors were doomed to spend their lives as slaves on the sugar plantations of the Caribbean and in the tobacco and cotton fields of America. When he recognized what a wretch he was, God's grace gave him hope and brought about his conversion. *Amazing Grace* is Newton's praise of God's mercy that could love even a slaver.

Newton recognized his sin and did not hide from his responsibility for it. He could seek and accept God's forgiving grace. How different from Adam and Eve!

Adam does not say, "Oh what a wretch I am! Yes, I have sinned." Instead, he tries to shift the blame to Eve and even to God. "The woman whom you put here with me — she gave me fruit from the tree, and so I ate it." *She* gave it to me, and *you* put her here, so it's not my fault, it's yours.

Eve does no better at accepting responsibility. For her, it's the serpent's fault. "The serpent tricked me into it, so I ate it."

From the first time we say, "It broke" as a child right through to the end of our lives, we do not want to take responsibility for the wrong we have done. Perhaps purgatory is the state in which we find ourselves while God waits for us to call ourselves wretches at last. We don't want to admit that we are at times wretches because the admission might make us wretched.

Of course, if we do not admit our wretchedness, we will not open ourselves to allowing God to embrace us, forgive us and welcome us into what St. Paul calls "a dwelling provided for us by God, a dwelling in the heavens, not made by hands, but to last forever."

That's where my problem starts. I want to experience the love of God, but I don't want to admit that I don't deserve it. I want God to love me because I am a good boy. So, I spend my life denying my sinfulness, wrapped up in my wretched self and refusing to accept the offer of God's love.

Is that the blasphemy against the Holy Spirit of which Jesus speaks? By refusing to accept God's love on its own terms, I sin against the Spirit of God who is love. That sin cannot be forgiven because it is a refusal to be forgiven. God won't force forgiveness on us.

There is no doubt about it: I am a wretch. And there is nothing I can do about it except accept that fact and turn to the Lord on his terms. Those terms are easy. All I have to do is admit that I am a wretch and accept God's strengthening forgiveness on the terms in which it is offered, unlimited love. Amazing grace!

Eleventh Sunday of the Year (B)

Today, St. Paul says, "We continue to be confident . . . We walk by faith, not by sight. I repeat, we are full of confidence."

What is it of which we are confident? The simple truth is that we are confident that God loves us, that the love of God is stronger than anything else in the universe and beyond it. We can sin, we can turn away, we can hide, we can die. Even so, the life-giving love of God will prevail.

So, there is nothing to be afraid of. Whatever happens to me, I will not be separated from God. Even if I were to lose my faith, God would still hold me near and dear.

Sounds a bit naive and even stupid, doesn't it? After all, there is plenty to be afraid of in this world. One needn't be neurotic or faithless to worry when crossing certain streets, let alone if living in an area prone to violence or natural disaster.

My faith is surrounded by doubts. The "bad guys" prosper. Children suffer. Thousands die in famines, floods, earthquakes and violence. Friends grow apart and relationships sour. I will die. Where can I find unambiguous proof of God's love for me? I doubt I can.

I cannot deny those doubts without being dishonest. Non-believers have an easier time of it. They can just say, "That's the way it is" and get on with their lives. We believers have to face the hard questions.

According to today's Gospel passage, Jesus recognizes the problem. He came to proclaim the Kingdom of God, but the evidence for it seemed slight, no greater than a mustard seed. Most of us would agree that it seems no bigger today.

The strange thing about Jesus's talking about the Kingdom as a mustard seed is that he intends that as encouragement. Why should I be encouraged to know that the fulfillment of God's action is barely visible? I want more than that. I want big-as-a-blimp certainty.

One reason for the ambiguity is the fact that God has chosen to make us the builders of the Kingdom. Its final fulfillment will be in

God's hands, but our cooperation and efforts are part of the building. Knowing that, and knowing us, makes it clearer why the signs of the Kingdom are ambiguous. I am ambiguous.

I am a child of God, a baptized Christian. That should make things pretty straightforward in how I live. But in practice, I do not live up to my Christian vocation. Sometimes, I am indistinguishable from anyone else.

Oh, I try. I go to church. I pray when I think of it. I read Scripture from time to time. I snatch a moment every so often for quiet reflection when I can't think of anything else to do. I try to at least avoid being nasty if I can't be nice. Not much more than a mustard seed's worth of Christian life.

At times, mustard seed is about as much as I can manage. That's discouraging. No wonder Jesus felt it necessary to speak of mustard seed as an encouragement.

Jesus says to me today, "Hey, don't sell yourself short. Your mustard seed is what the Reign of God is about. Your little faith, your little effort is enough. Give your little bit and stand by amazed as you see what God will do with it. Your mustard seed will flourish."

Twelfth Sunday of the Year (B)

A hospitalized woman said to me, "I'm afraid to sleep at night."
"Why?"
"The doctors won't tell me, but I know I'm dying."
She was right. She was dying, and the doctors had not yet told her. But, she knew.

It was her knowledge that she would die soon that made her afraid to sleep. Sleeping required a lack of fear and a willingness to let go that she did not yet have.

Going to sleep is certainly a risk. While I am unconscious, the world continues on its course. All sorts of things happen and I neither know nor control them. I am even personally vulnerable. Closing my eyes for a nap or a night is an almost foolhardy act of daring.

The night prayer of the Church recognizes the connection between sleep and death. Our night prayers are meant to be a preparation both for dropping off to sleep and for death, when we will have to let go of everything. Every night, the prayer ends with the wish, "May the all-powerful Lord grant us a restful night and a peaceful death." We're supposed to close our eyes at night as if we were practicing to die.

We need a faith that can sleep. We don't often think of faith as something to sleep about. Prayer, action, study, reflection, proclamation — that's what we think faith means. Doing nothing? Sleeping? Is that faith, too?

In the Gospel, the disciples are all very busy. There is a terrific storm raging. They are awake in a nightmare, doing all the things required to prevent their boat's swamping and their drowning. Meanwhile, Jesus is asleep.

Finally, the disciples can bear it no longer. They wake Jesus and give him one of the few bawlings out he receives from the disciples: "Teacher, doesn't it matter to you that we are going to drown?" They are literally all in the same boat. If the disciples fail in their efforts to keep it afloat, they and Jesus will drown. No wonder they are upset with him for sleeping while they are busy panicking. They are facing death and he's snoring!

Why was that? An obvious answer is that he must have been exhausted. But, that's not answer enough. Perhaps the disciples were right and he just didn't care. After all, they would all die sooner or later anyway, so what's the fuss? Maybe he was just so fed up with the disciples and frustrated with his own mission that he just wished it would all go away. Maybe he was sleeping as a means of escape.

Or, maybe Jesus had a sleeper's faith. Perhaps his trust in God was such that he was able to let go, to relinquish control over his life and events and leave it all to God. He could take the risk of going to sleep, a sound enough sleep to be undisturbed by a raging storm, because he knew that God was on watch.

Jesus could sleep because he knew that God does not sleep. He could afford to let go, to let the world move along, because he knew it will never move beyond the loving care of God. Even in a storm, even in his sleep of death on the Cross Jesus knew that God's watchful care is present.

The same is true for me. When I am asleep I am no less embraced by God's love than when I am awake.

Does that mean that while I sleep there will be no storms, there will be no monsters hiding under my bed? Of course not. There will be. Faith does not scare away the nightmares. It makes us confident that the worst they can do to us will not overcome God's love. That's true as well for the biggest nightmare of them all, death.

So, each night we prepare to sleep by recalling our day, by reminding ourselves that God will bring our efforts to fruition and by making the big act of faith — we close our eyes.

Thirteenth Sunday of the Year (B)

What kind of person thinks there are destructive drugs in the world? What would you call someone who insists that corpses are dead? "A realist," right?

Today's first reading denies the existence of destructive drugs and in the Gospel Jesus tells mourners that the dead girl in front of them is asleep.

Are believers not realists? Do we live in a world of make-believe, refusing to accept facts?

That is a question we must not avoid. And the answer is not a once-for-all exercise. Each day, we are faced with facts that should call into question our faith in God.

The philosopher Miguel de Unamuno said, "Faith that does not doubt is dead faith." An untested, unchallenged faith is not faith at all, but a wilful refusal to inhabit this universe rather than a world of make-believe.

So, what are we to make of our readings today? Are the realists right or is faith right?

Perhaps the real question is: "What is reality?"

The "realist" is someone who uses a commonsense approach to life. If science and the evidence of our senses indicate that something is real, then it is real. By the same token, what cannot be verified by those means is unreal. Can't see or measure God? Then, God either does not exist or is irrelevant.

But, is this realism? "Realists" accuse believers of avoiding reality, but might we not say that it is the "realist" who avoids reality, who cannot accept what will never fit inside human concepts or understanding? Perhaps the atheist is the one who cannot accept reality because it won't fit into a human head.

So then, what is reality? An easy answer for the believer is to say that what God wills is real and that anything that goes against the divine will, no matter how obvious to us, is basically unreal.

In that case, dangerous drugs and death and sin and injustice and all manner of evil are unreal because they are not the will of God. Today's reading from Wisdom says that. "Through the devil's envy death entered the world; and those who belong to his company experience it."

It is an attractive idea. But, is it too easy? If only the things God wills as good are real, then what do we make of the Cross of Christ and his call to take up our own crosses to follow him? No, we cannot deny the reality of pain, suffering, evil and death in the world. We cannot claim that only those who belong to the devil experience them. They are not the whole reality, but they are a real part of it.

So, the world as God wills it and the world as we experience it are both real. To accept only one while ignoring the other is not realistic. The atheist and the other-worldly believer are of the same ilk.

It is by accepting the co-reality of good and evil that the Christian is the true realist.

Our advantage is the Cross. The Cross is the place where the highest reality, God, and the lowest reality, evil, come together. By embracing death, Christ makes all reality a way to God.

Because I am a realist who believes that God loves me, I can accept the other realities of my life. I suffer, I sin and I will die. But because reality involves the love of God, I can be confident that my suffering is united with God's suffering, that my sins are forgiven and that my death is a sleep that through God's love will lead to the fullness of reality.

Fourteenth Sunday of the Year (B)

When I was a seminarian I decided I no longer wanted to believe in God. I was training in a hospital, and I still went through the motions while making a final decision to quit.

One day, as I walked into a room to visit a Catholic, the other patient in the room cried out, "Hallelujah, Praise Jesus!"

I was in no mood for evangelical Christianity, so I merely nodded and went to the bed of the Catholic patient, where I spent most of the time trying to figure out how to get out of the room without having to deal with the "holy roller." I stood up and tried to quickly leave the room. I failed.

"Reverend, Jesus is wonderful! Come over here and let's talk." I was too polite or cowardly to say, "Listen, Lady, I'm just going through the motions until I decide for sure to leave all this God business, so leave me alone."

The woman talked about Jesus, and how she trusted in him to heal the arthritis that had her totally crippled. She could not stand, walk or use her hands. Whenever she said Jesus was wonderful, I would just say, "Uh-huh." Finally, I was able to escape. As I left, she made me promise to come back in the afternoon.

I spent lunch and the class after it dreading facing her again. But, a promise is a promise, so I dragged myself back to the ward. Fortunately, when I arrived, there was an emergency, so I had an excuse to not go back to the "Bible bouncer."

The next time I was at the hospital, I steeled myself to make the visit I hadn't made that afternoon. Sure enough, as soon as I walked into the room, I was greeted with, "Hallelujah, Praise Jesus!"

"The other afternoon, I kept waiting for you to come, but you didn't. I just kept looking at the chair you sat in, and wondered where you were. Then I realized that you were bringing the love of Jesus to someone else. I remembered that when you were here and we talked, the love of Jesus was with us, and that love could heal me and I could walk. So, I got up out of this bed to go to the toilet. I saw a nurse in the hall, and she said, 'What are you doing out of bed? You can't walk!' And I said, 'The Reverend was here and the love of Jesus was with us, so I can walk.' And the nurse said, 'Oh, OK, but don't overdo it.'" (I love that response.)

Four days later, I visited the hospital again, this time looking forward to seeing that woman. I saw her, alright. She walked up to me in the lobby, thanked me for healing her and told me she had come to visit patients.

What is the relationship between faith and miracle? Certainly the only faith in that hospital room was hers, not mine. Because she believed, a miracle could happen. She could walk and I could believe.

God does not force us to accept love. In today's Gospel, we hear that Jesus could not perform miracles because people would not believe in him. They were not willing to accept the love God offered them because it came in a form they did not expect. A carpenter? A home-town boy? No wonder "they found him too much for them." They wanted something more dramatic, but they got the local carpenter, just as all I got was an old "Bible bouncer."

That woman believed, and so the love of God could work miracles. What is hope-giving is that her faith was sufficient to cure one without faith. God was willing to work through her faith to heal the two of us.

Perhaps that is why we live our faith in a community called "Church." We need each other's faith in order to believe. We support the weak with our faith, and when we are weak, the community will carry us to the Lord. Even when I doubt, I must hold to that community, even if I think I cannot hold to God. Being with believers puts us at risk of miracles.

I still don't know what happened in that hospital room. I know God did something, but I'm not sure what. All I know is that the faith of one made a miracle happen for two and a woman who could not walk has carried me for more than forty years.

Fifteenth Sunday of the Year (B)

Jesus gave his disciples many commands: "Love one another," "Go into the whole world," "Receive the Holy Spirit." But in today's Gospel passage, he gives a command that doesn't seem to make much sense.

When he sent the disciples out, Jesus told them to wear sandals. Telling them to not carry an extra tunic makes some sense if he wants them to live simply. But why tell them to make sure they have their footwear on? Surely there must be more important things to be said.

Many people go through life without ever wearing shoes. Feet can be tough. Through most of our evolutionary past we were all barefoot. It is only in extreme situations that we really need footwear — ice fields, coal mines, city sidewalks.

The shoe that says what "shoe-ness" is all about may be the steel-toed boot of the construction worker. "Protection." That is what shoes are, protection for our feet as we go about our tasks.

Protection for the sake of a task may be the reason the Lord tells us to make sure we're properly shod when going forth to share the Good News.

Our vocation as Christians is the most vital in the world. Billions of our brothers and sisters live without knowing "the God and Father of our Lord Jesus Christ who has bestowed on us every spiritual blessing in the heavens!" Those men and women have the right to know that. The way God has chosen to give them that Good News is the Church, you and me and all the disciples of Christ in every land and time.

That is an urgent task, and nothing should interfere with it. On a stroll from Jerusalem to Jericho, a thorn in the foot might be an inconvenience. In the spread of the Gospel, the delay is disastrous.

Our life as Christians is that urgent, that important to the world. I am essential to the world and my life as a Christian is too important to the world for me to be sidetracked by sore feet. So, the Lord says, "Wear sandals."

Can that really be the case? Am I really that important to the world?

Appearances, inclinations and desires to the contrary notwithstanding, it is true. I am essential to the life of the world. I am one of the heralds of the Gospel, whether at home or on the road. My mission is too important to let any problems or concerns of my own (the emotional, social, or even spiritual versions of thorns in the foot) sidetrack me.

It is hard to believe that God is relying upon me, when I thought I was supposed to rely upon God. But that's the case. God needs me, needs us, to bring the Good News to a world waiting unawares for it. So Jesus tells us to wear our shoes, ready to go forth and ready to be ready.

That means more than just wearing Birkenstocks, Nikes or Pradas. It means I should be aware of possible obstacles to living my mission and make provision for them.

Do I lack the words to put my faith into ways others will understand? Study the Word of God and the message of the Church. Do I lack confidence in myself? Unite with the community of believers in worship and sacrament. Am I a sinner? Repent, confess and receive forgiveness. Am I unsure of the way? Serve. Am I afraid? Pray and keep moving.

Perhaps that is the real message of Jesus in commanding his disciples to wear sandals: keep moving, keep being ready to move. Your message, your life is too important to the world for delay.

Sixteenth Sunday of the Year (B)

I went to a monastery because though I was very active and talked a good deal about the Christian life, prayer and a sense of God's love were missing in my life. I asked the prior if one of the monks could give me some direction during my week there. His answer was "No."

"You don't need guidance. You're a busy man, working hard for the Gospel. Too hard, perhaps. No, you don't need guidance beyond this: Sleep. Get up for meals and then go back to bed. If you want to come to our community prayers, you are welcome, but don't get out of bed for them. When you find you can no longer sleep or rest because you no longer need them, then you'll know what to do. After all, you're a priest, you tell others how to live a Christian life."

So, I slept for three days, after which I told the prior I was relaxed and comfortable. So, he sent me into the orchard to help the novices pick fruit and do other work that would let my mind rest. I have met many wise men and women; he is one of the wisest.

In today's Gospel passage, Jesus gives the same advice to the apostles. He had sent them out to heal and teach. They have returned to him excited and full of stories about all they had been doing and all that God had been doing through them. So, he commands them, "Come by yourselves to an out-of-the-way place and rest a little."

God is not a taskmaster. In the view of eternity, what need has God of time cards to track my every moment and make sure I am giving full value for the divine investment in my creation? Can God who created monkeys and kittens (and ridiculous me) be all that serious? Can the Creator who allowed billions of years for life to evolve really be anxious that I be working all the time, busy all the time?

I suspect part of my problem is a lack of trust in God. Deep down, I fear that if I am not doing something at every waking moment (and staying awake nights to get it done or at least to worry about it), things will not happen as they should. If I were not on duty, the whole universe would be lost.

Certainly God has expectations of me. There is a vocation I have been given that no other man or woman can fulfil. But, I cannot live that vocation if I am so anxious, so busy, so driven that I forget that ultimately the work is God's. Nor can I live it if I am too busy to take time simply to be quiet and hear what the Lord might be trying to say to me through the din of my activity.

Why not from time to time take the time to stop my efforts, to realize that even when I am not running about doing what I think God and the universe need, God will still be caring for, loving and giving life to the world?

There are, perhaps, people for whom life is such that they never need an honest break. Either their life is so grace-filled that their everyday activities are spirit-renewing, or they never do anything that leaves them in need of rest. I am neither.

The apostles and, more than we suspect, most of us are busy in our own ways. We serve, we pray, we study, we serve some more. We do.

So, the Lord tells the apostles and us to pack up the picnic basket, get in the boat and get away from it all. Our bodies, minds and souls all need an occasional break.

Sometimes, to find prayer and God's love, all I need do is not do.

Seventeenth Sunday of the Year (B)

The story of Jesus feeding the crowd is the only miracle account that appears in all four Gospels. Early Christians obviously considered this an important story, one that could not be left out of any account of our faith.

The reason is plain to see when we look at what Jesus does. He takes bread, gives thanks and shares it with the people, who then eat it. Those are the four hallmark gestures of the Eucharist: taking, blessing, breaking and sharing. The story teaches us that the Eucharist is real food for those who follow Christ, and that there is no limit to its ability to feed us or to the number of people for whom it is meant.

Jesus is, of course, the center of the story, but I once saw a children's book that gave a big place to the boy who had the loaves and fish. In fact, he never actually appears. Andrew talks about him, and that's all.

There are two other people in today's account whom it would be easy to overlook. Yet I think they provide an opportunity to put myself into the story in a way that Jesus and the boy do not. I am not a miracle worker. I do not often have exactly what is needed like the boy. Granted, I have needs like the crowd, but I can't identify with a crowd. Philip and Andrew, though, fit me.

Philip is in an uncomfortable position. Jesus looks to him and says, in effect, "We have an impossible situation here. What are you going to do about it?" Philip has been a follower of Jesus from the start. He has come to look to Jesus for leadership and for signs of God's power. It must have been a shock, then, to have the Lord turn to him for a solution, asking, "Where shall we buy bread for these people to eat?"

Philip gives the answer most of us would give. "Not even with two hundred day's wages could we buy loaves enough to give each of them a mouthful!" He sees the size of the problem, recognizes his small abilities, does an analysis of the situation and decides that nothing can be done. Very smart. Very prudent.

Philip and I have a lot in common. I, too, try to be smart. I look around at my world and evaluate the problems and situations I see. I hear the Lord saying, "We have an impossible situation here. What are you going to do about it?" I look at my own abilities and weaknesses, count up the number of hours in a day, think it all over, and answer as Philip: "No can do!" Very smart. Very prudent.

But there's Andrew to look at as well. Andrew has looked at the same situation. He knows the size of the problem. However, rather than admit defeat, he looks for what can be done. So, he comes to Jesus and says, "There is a lad here who has five barley loaves and a couple of dried fish, but what good is that for so many?" He knows that nothing much can be done, but he is at least on the lookout, keeping his eyes open for anything that might alleviate the situation.

Andrew does not offer much, but it is enough for the Lord to work a miracle. He did what little he could, and everyone ate.

There are times when I am like Andrew. There is not much I can do, but, I can do something. I can remain sensitive to the world's needs and alert to all that might answer those needs.

The Eucharist is the miracle in which Christ takes "the work of human hands" and presents it to the Father as himself. Our own little bit, our own willingness to search out what we can do, becomes part of that. God is looking for the Andrew in each of us.

Eighteenth Sunday of the Year (B)

Jesus says, "No one who comes to me shall ever be hungry, no one who comes to me shall ever thirst again."

Well, we gather to share the Eucharist. But, when I leave the celebration, I want a bite to eat. Feasting on Word and Sacrament does not lessen my need for ordinary food and drink. Has Jesus lied to us?

An obvious answer is that the Lord was not talking about physical hunger. He is speaking of spiritual hungers, and he is the answer to them.

But my spiritual hungers remain. I know I am not alone. Many, maybe all, Christians, feel a famine of the spirit.

We are hungry, and probably will remain so throughout life. In fact, it seems that the more we grow as Christians, the more hungry we get. So the problem remains: was Jesus lying to us when he said that those who come to him would never feel hunger or thirst?

Since the Lord spoke in terms of physical hunger, let's take a look at it. Two kinds of people are hungry. The obvious ones are those who have gone without eating for some time. The time may be only that between breakfast and a morning coffee break, or it may be a prolonged period of starvation.

The second group is those who eat even when they have no physical need: compulsive eaters, food addicts, gluttons. It does not matter to them what they eat, or they prefer non-nourishing foods to healthful ones.

When I was a boy, my aunt took me to a well-known restaurant. I was too young to appreciate the menu, so I asked for a hamburger and french fries. Throughout the rest of her life, Aunt Sally joked that faced with a choice of fine foods, I chose a burger.

I wonder if my unfilled spiritual hunger is the kind I had that day. The Lord offers to feed me, but perhaps I am so full of spiritual junk food and looking for more of the same that I do not and cannot take in the nourishment the Lord actually presents. I don't know what's good for me because I don't recognize real food.

What is spiritual junk food? It's different things to different people. For one, it might be a job. For another, beauty. For yet another, glamor or status. For some, it might even be religiosity.

How can I discover what my junk food might be? What can't I do without? What am I willing to make sacrifices to have? The odds are that those things are not real nourishment for the depths of my being.

If I decide to become hungry, giving up junk, I can be filled by God, who comes to me when I decide to open myself in prayer, reflection and service. When I start to feel real hunger for God's presence, I no longer look at myself. I begin to see my sisters and brothers who are also in need of physical or spiritual nourishment. I serve them, and find myself feeling hunger for the presence and grace of God. Then, as I continue my service, I feel a growing sense that I am indeed being fed by the Lord, cared for by the Lord, loved by the Lord.

The Lord sets a banquet before me, but all too often, I look over, under and around the table for the sort of nourishment I think I need instead of feasting on what I am offered, the only real nourishment I need.

Nineteenth Sunday of the Year (B)

Elijah destroyed the prophets of idolatry, and Queen Jezebel vowed, "So may the gods do to me, and more also, if I do not make your life like the life of one of them by this time tomorrow."

So, Elijah high-tails it into the desert. He's had enough. He just wants to lie down and die. But, the Lord has other plans. An angel awakens Elijah and gives him food and drink. Elijah decides to top off the meal with another nap, but the angel tells him to eat and drink some more and get on the road. So, Elijah gets up and travels 40 days and nights to the mountain of God.

There are details in the story that are symbolic. Ever since it took 40 years for the Hebrews to reach the promised land from Egypt, the number came to mean "a very long time." Whatever the actual number, Elijah went through the wilderness for a very long time.

Another detail is Elijah's destination, Mount Horeb. By Elijah's day, the Hebrews lived in two kingdoms. For people in Israel, God's revelation to Moses took place on Mount Sinai. In Judah, home of Elijah, the site was called Mount Horeb. So, Elijah headed off to the place of God's revelation.

So, what does it mean to say that Elijah journeyed for 40 days to Horeb after eating the food the angel gave him? It means that he spent a long time on the road to meet God, but was sustained on that journey by the strength of God.

I have a lot in common with Elijah. I have times when it seems that all my efforts are useless, that the world is too much to handle. Even if I don't wish I were dead, I want to crawl into bed and pull the blanket up over my head.

But, that's not all I have in common with Elijah. Like him, I am on a journey for which I need help, the equivalent of the special foods of explorers and adventurers. It is a journey that passes through the wilderness of my own pain and sin as well as the pain and sin of the world. It is a journey that will last my whole lifetime. It is the journey to God.

50

Elijah had hearth cake and a jug of water to sustain him. What of me on my journey?

Jesus says, "I am the living bread that came down from heaven. Whoever eats of this bread will live forever; and the bread I will give for the life of the world is my flesh."

The Eucharist we share is food like that the angel gave Elijah. It is food that enables us to persevere in our long journey to God. It is the strength of God.

In the Eucharist, we have an advantage over Elijah. The food he ate gave him energy for the journey. The "bread that comes down from heaven, so that one who eats it will not die" is more. It is not only bread for us on the way, it is Jesus, the Way and the Destination of our life's journey. In a sense, we are at our destination before we arrive there.

We share the Eucharist, and go about our daily lives empowered like the prophet who reached the mountain of God. Knowing the end of our journey, we travel confidently through this world, aiding our sisters and brothers who may not yet know the way, may not yet realize that the bread of angels is available to them.

Elijah ate the angel's food cake and reached the mountain of God. The Hebrews ate manna in the desert, and reached the promised land. We eat the bread of life and reach eternal life with God.

Twentieth Sunday of the Year (B)

Early Christians were accused of atheism because we did not worship the gods. We were accused of being antisocial because we formed tight-knit communities. We were accused of treason because we did not pay proper respect to the authorities and refused to serve in the army. We were accused of immorality because our major gathering was called a "love feast." Perhaps the most interesting charge was cannibalism.

Where did anyone get the idea that Christians are cannibals? They probably got it from us, and we got it from Jesus. He claims to be living bread. When the crowd gets squeamish, he says, "if you do not eat the flesh of the Son of Man and drink his blood, you have no life in you . . . for my flesh is real food and my blood real drink."

We are so used to hearing "The Body of Christ . . . The Blood of Christ" that we forget how shocking they are, though some years ago, a popular hymn had the refrain, "Eat his body, drink his blood." followed by a pause before the next phrase long enough for some to insert the word "Yuck!"

Early Christians did not hesitate to say the Eucharist really is the body and blood of the Lord. What we later came to call the "Real Presence" was so real to them that they spoke forthrightly about eating and drinking the Lord.

Over the centuries, Christians have tried to explain how bread and wine could be the body and blood of the Lord, but no explanation can be completely satisfying. Since the Middle Ages, Catholics have used a theory called *transubstantiation*. This explanation has waned in popularity because it relies upon philosophy as taught by Aristotle some 350 years before Christ. People attuned to contemporary science and philosophy find the medieval explanation either inadequate or incomprehensible.

Ultimately, the *how* of the Eucharist is not important. What is important is that the Lord said his body and blood are real food, that the bread and wine of the Eucharist are that body and blood, and that we are to remember him by sharing the Eucharist.

For us, remembering is an intellectual activity, though our senses may be involved as well when, for example, an aroma sparks memories.

In Scripture, however, remembering is something more. To remember something is to make it real once again. At Passover, Jews remember the Exodus by talking not about their ancestors 32 centuries ago, but about themselves as escapees from Egypt. They affirm that in remembering Moses and the Hebrews, they, too, are liberated from bondage.

You may have noticed the same style when I spoke about accusations against Christians in the second century as accusations against us. If you remember an event in salvation history, you enter it. It is really present. And so are you.

Thus, when Jesus tells us to "do this in remembrance of me," he is not enjoining some intellectual activity or nostalgia for some "once upon a time." He is saying, "enter the reality of being with me, meet the real me, eat the bread and wine that are my presence among you." The Eucharist we share really is Christ present among us, present for us.

Outsiders might not understand. In a sense, neither do we. We believe. We believe that Christ is with us in our Eucharistic celebration. We believe that his presence is not merely something that happens in our memories. We believe that he shares himself with us so that we may live as he did, proclaiming and being the love of God for the world.

Would someone watching us at the Eucharist be so stirred or disturbed by my conviction that the sacrament is the real presence of Christ for me that he or she might think I was involved in some form of cannibalism?

Twenty-First Sunday of the Year (B)

When Jesus said that the Eucharist is really his body, "from this time on, many of his disciples broke away and would not remain in his company any longer."

So long as Jesus gave inspiring talks and good moral advice, made trenchant comments about the religious establishment and worked wonders, people were happy to follow him.

There is no shortage of such people. Some admire Jesus as a moral teacher. Some paint him as a political challenger of the "system" of his time. Some make him into a sort of mystical figure who taught esoteric knowledge to an enlightened elite. Some make him out to be a wonder worker who relieves us of responsibility for our world because he will one day fix it. Still others consider him a powerful god who play-acted at being human.

They share something with the disciples who left Jesus. They find him too big. He doesn't fit their categories and understanding, but goes beyond them. Rather than face a reality that transcends their ideas of who he should be, they leave.

They and we are faced with the fact that Jesus is more than we can feel comfortable with. If he were merely a moral teacher, that would be fine. We would have him under our control because we could understand him.

If, on the other hand, Jesus were some remote divinity we would still be able to contain him. "Totally Other" is something I can understand, it fits into my head. It means "Not me." No connection, and therefore no need to take him into account beyond, perhaps, going through an occasional ritual to make sure a volcano doesn't erupt in my living room. I could box him, and put the box far away.

Our problem, and the problem of those disciples who left him, is that Jesus refuses to be either totally one of us or totally a remote divinity. He talks about ascending "to where he was before." He claims divinity. But, he also claims to be with us in a piece of bread and a cup of wine, a claim that the Church makes the center of its life and worship.

Divinity that fits our preconceptions is nice, but beyond them it becomes scary, especially if it gets as close as the Eucharist. We are not in control. We want either a domesticated or a distant god. Jesus is undomesticated, and in my hand! It's like being in a cage with a tiger.

When Jesus turned to Peter and the rest of the Twelve, he in effect asked them if they were willing to live with such knowledge. Could they endure the thought that God, the all-powerful, was with them, asking them questions, offering himself as food?

Peter's answer is an acceptance of the facts. "Where else could we go? If you are who you say, then there is no place else we could go and still live in the real world."

If Jesus is indeed who he and the Church say he is, then there really is no place else to go. If he is real, then any alternative is unreal. We have no choice. If we accept the truth of Jesus' divinity, we must accept the reality of the Eucharist we share.

Many that day could be disciples until Jesus started talking about being as intimate with us and familiar to us as a bite of bread and a sip of wine. Our gathering each week is a proclamation to the world and to one another that what he said then is true today. He was, is and always will be God with us.

Twenty-Second Sunday of the Year (B)

One result of the Church's move into the Roman Empire and beyond was that the Biblical background of Christians was replaced with a pagan one.

Jewish Christians came to the Church a with view of God and traditions connected to the history of God's relationship with the Chosen People.

Christians with a pagan background carried their own customs and ways of thinking into the Church. Many of them, like Greek philosophy and most of our Christmas customs, enriched the Church. Many, like certain attitudes towards saints and relics, presented problems. Most were probably both blessings and curses.

As the Church continues to spread throughout the world, attitudes that differ from Biblical thought continue to enter our way of viewing God and the world. Some enrich us. Some present problems. Some do both.

The difficulty is that we tend to take those attitudes for granted, and fail to measure them against the Scripture and the teaching of the Church. They are so much a part of us that we don't even notice it. I wonder if some of my own attitudes about God can be traced to my horse-sacrificing ancestors in Europe long ago.

In this week's passage from Mark, the Pharisees point out that Jesus' disciples don't follow the customs of their ancestors, and as their master, Jesus is responsible for what they do or fail to do.

Because of their negative portrayal in the gospels, we may forget that the Pharisees were very devout believers who tried to shape every aspect of their lives with reference to their faith. They did not consider following various practices as a replacement for faith. Bringing those practices into their everyday life protected their faith, made it a part of everything they did, even washing their hands before meals.

So, what was the problem? What's wrong with having practices that allow faith to be part of everything we do? After all, we have the custom of praying before meals to remind ourselves that all that we have comes from God, and that the meals we share with others are related to the Eucharistic banquet we share with the whole Church.

There is nothing wrong with those customs. The problem appears when we make particular customs a measure of someone else's faith, or even our own. Because his disciples did not follow certain customs, the Pharisees assumed that Jesus was not a man of true faith.

This brings us back to the practices we have inherited from the cultures and religions our community has met and welcomed through the centuries. Those practices can help make our faith more than an intellectual exercise. They can help us understand God's works and help us actually do something on a regular basis about that understanding.

However, there are two reasons we must always be ready to examine our devotional practices.

The first is that how we show our faith eventually shapes our faith. So, we must always match the practices of our faith with the content of our faith. Do my devotions, practices and thoughts deepen my understanding of real Christianity, or am I in danger of wandering from the truth? Have the customs I learned from my family, from my community and from the teachers of my faith begun to warp or replace that faith?

The second reason I must examine my practices is that I might otherwise inflate their value and decide that all Christians must pray and practice as I do. I will then be like the Pharisees who presumed to know the quality of Jesus' faith by what he and his disciples did or didn't do.

The Church has been, when all is said and done, enriched by a careful openness to many ways to express our faith. As individuals, we must be as open, but as careful.

Twenty-Third Sunday of the Year (B)

Jesus went through several actions in curing the deaf man in today's gospel. He touched the man's ears, spat, and touched his tongue. "Then he looked up to heaven and groaned."

We tend to look upon the Cross as something that happened at the end of Jesus' ministry. The gospels, however, were written under the shadow of the Cross. Every event in the life of Jesus portrayed in the gospels is connected to the Cross.

Was the groan of Jesus when he cured that man a groan from the Cross?

One of the amazing things about us human beings is that we think that there is something wrong with the world. We think it is supposed to be a different place. Why do we do that?

Why do we feel that something is wrong when children get ill? After all, disease and death are natural.

Why do we think there should be fairness, and even some special breaks for the weaker among us? What about the survival of the fittest?

Why do we feel that accidents are evil, or that volcanoes, earthquakes and typhoons should not occur? This is the planet we live on, and there is no other available.

Something within us rebels against the facts. We may not be able to say what we think the world should be, but we know we don't want what we've got.

In other words, we have a hunger for salvation. We desire to be freed for something better. Christians know the source of our desire is the fact that God has created us to share in the life of the Trinity. We also know that the frustration of that desire has its foundation in sin. We may not be sure of the how, but we know it to be the case, and we know that we are not capable of freeing ourselves from the power and effects of sin.

Whatever healing there is of our separation from God and from each other, whatever answer there will be to our desire for a different world, comes only through Christ and what he did on the Cross. The important point is that there is no other way to bring about salvation. It's the Cross or nothing.

That means that all healing of the world's ills must share in the cross in some way. Therefore, when Jesus healed the deaf man who could not speak, he was in some sense doing the work of the Cross. That is the reason for his groan. That healing was part and parcel of the healing, the salvation, that Jesus achieved on the Cross.

What implications does that have for me? Does it mean that if I decide to do more than wish this were a better world I had better expect to groan? Is the only way to fix the broken world to allow myself to be broken?

Have you ever wondered why the Cross is the symbol of Christianity? The empty tomb could have been. The Ascension could have been. So many comforting and glorious things could have been. But, we use the Cross. It is on our churches, it is in our homes, it is marked on our bodies when we are baptized and we renew the mark each time we pray.

The answer, then, is one we knew all along. The way to make God's love present in this creation is to groan with Christ. Anyone who has tried to share God's love with the world comes to know that. Our willingness to groan, to offer real healing to the world, will be the salvation of the world. Our groans will lead to a Resurrection.

Twenty-Fourth Sunday of the Year (B)

Once upon a time, there was a woman who had lived a long life. It wasn't a bad life. She had her share of joys and achievements, of love, friendship and family.

But, as life continued, she also had pains and sorrows. In other words, the woman had a cross to bear. She admitted that it was not a big one, but she still felt that it might not be the right one for her. It seemed to be getting too heavy.

So, one day she went to heaven and demanded a different cross. Saint Peter was surprised, but he asked an angel to escort her inside so she could find a cross she felt fitted her better.

The angel led her to a warehouse.

"What's this?" the woman asked.

"This is the cross warehouse," said the angel. "Everyone who comes here lays his or her cross down before going farther in. You should be able to find one here that suits you."

So the woman began shopping around. One time, she thought she'd try on an attractive little thing, not too small, but compact enough to not be a strain. However, when she tried lifting it, she realized that it was made of lead. She realized that looking at someone else's cross does not tell us how heavy it might be.

For the fun of it, she then tried a big cross that would certainly attract attention. But, though it looked big, it was so light that she would have been embarrassed to bear it.

In the meantime, the angel was getting impatient. It was after hours, and there's no overtime pay for angels.

Just when the angel was about to lose all patience, the woman finally picked up one cross near the door and said, "Ah, this is the one. Good fit, heavy enough to be an honest-to-God cross, but not too much for me to handle."

The angel exploded, "Lady, that's the cross you came here with!"

Cross-bearing seems an inescapable part of human life. Jesus tells us to welcome our cross, confident that no matter how painful it might be, God's love will not be overwhelmed.

But, the question remains. Why must we carry a cross at all? After all, a cross is not pleasant. It really is a torture to face the big crosses of our lives. Couldn't God just get rid of them for us? Wasn't it enough that Jesus bore his cross? If he's our savior, why wasn't his crucifixion enough to cover for all of us? What good does a cross do me?

There must be something about the cross in itself that has value. After all, the Church has always said that it is the cross, not the empty tomb, that saves.

One of the key messages of the prophets is that God suffers. God is heartbroken over what people do to one another and to themselves when they abandon love. When God came among us, the suffering of God and the suffering of humanity were united in Jesus. The crosses we bear do not merely bring us close to God, they make us like God, God who suffers.

Does this mean that suffering is good and we should seek it out for ourselves and not strive to ease it for others? No, suffering is not God's will for the world. The suffering of the world breaks God's heart.

Christ's call for us to take up the cross is an invitation to learn that though suffering is always with us and may make us think God is far from us, it is actually a share in the life of God who also takes up the cross.

Twenty-Fifth Sunday of the Year (B)

Even though the Gospel of John ends with the declaration "there are many other things that Jesus did," we tend to think we have the whole story just as it occurred with nothing left out, no pieces moved around. We haven't.

The gospel writers took reminiscences about Jesus and stories about what he had done and said. Then, they picked and chose among them and put them together to make their narratives suit the needs of the communities for which they wrote.

It's like a quilter who takes different pieces of cloth and puts them together to make a single quilt. In some sections, the seams are barely visible because the pieces look similar. In other sections, the fact that adjoining pieces are very different makes the match-up obvious.

In this week's passage from Mark, the seam is easy to see. In the first section, Jesus and the disciples are going through Galilee, and he talks about his death and resurrection. Then, presumably at some other time, though in the text it appears to follow immediately upon the Galilee walk, the disciples are in the Capernaum area, talking about who is most important. Considering the unlikelihood of the disciples wanting first place after being told that the way of Christ is a way to death, as well as the differences in time and place, the seam becomes obvious.

Why would Mark (or whoever he got the story from) put these two particular pieces together? Why did he think that they were an appropriate match, even that they must be together? What is the connection between the death and resurrection of Jesus, arguments about importance and the welcoming of a child?

We can all understand the argument the disciples had. We spend much of our lives seeking status, protecting our status, or mourning the loss of status.

It is as if my value as a human being depends upon outdoing others. The child's cry, "Me first!" is the simplest declaration of what it is about. I am self-centered. I worship a false god, one that has my name and face. So long as I serve that god, I am handicapped in meeting the one true God.

That, perhaps, is the reason Jesus says that welcoming a child is welcoming "the One who sent me." There is something that happens in that sort of meeting that moves my focus off myself and allows me to meet God.

At the time of Jesus, children had no legal rights, and were not generally taken into account in the lives of adults or society. They were powerless, lower in status than any adult. For an adult to greet a child, to welcome one's company, would be demeaning.

Yet, that is what Jesus says his disciples must do. They must step down from the pedestals they build for themselves and welcome the unimportant, the overlooked, the powerless. If they do that, they will meet God.

Who might the overlooked be today? There is no shortage: refugees, the poor, abused children, the uneducated, minorities, persons with AIDS, youth, the elderly, prisoners, the disabled, the unbelievers — we need only stop looking at ourselves to find them.

What has this to do, however, with the first piece of patchwork, Jesus' comments about his death and resurrection?

Mark apparently wants us to see that being willing to shift our focus from ourselves to meet the overlooked, to welcome them into our lives, is one of the ways we imitate Christ. It is as if after writing the passage about Jesus talking of his death, Mark asked himself, "What does this mean for our lives as Christians today?"

Twenty-Sixth Sunday of the Year (B)

Most people who have ever lived have not been followers of Jesus. Most have never even heard of him.

So, are most of our ancestors separated from Christ in death as they seemed to be in life? Are most people alive today separated in the same way? Must one be a Christian to be embraced by the life-giving Spirit of God? There are Christians, some of them Catholics, who say that is so.

In Mark's Gospel, John has a problem because God's saving work is apparently not confined to "insiders": "Teacher, we saw a man using your name to expel demons and we tried to stop him because he is not of our company." John felt that the work of Christ in healing, forgiving and sharing the love of God was a possession of those who called themselves his followers, "our company."

Jesus answers that, "Anyone who is not against us is for us." Those who do the will of God, whether they know Christ explicitly or not, or whether or not they are part of his "company" — the Church — or not, are cooperating with Christ in making the Reign of God present in our world.

Even atheists can serve in building the Kingdom. It does not depend solely upon us Christians. God will bring it about through many people, cultures and events.

That is good news for us as we look at a world in which most people will never know of Jesus Christ, let alone become his followers. It is a comfort to think that they and the thousands of men and women who are our ancestors all have a place in God's plan.

In fact, "outsiders" may be important to us in our vocation.

The original company of believers betrayed Christ. They deserted him when he was arrested and killed.

We are capable of similar betrayal. The history of the Church includes horrifying events and actions that can receive no justification, only forgiveness. My own life, too, contains no shortage of betrayal of my vocation as a Christian. At times, we Christians must be confronted with our sin and be challenged to fidelity. Frequently, it is outsiders who render that service to God and us.

So, men and women who are "not of our company" have several roles to play in building the Kingdom of God. God's love draws them to a sort of faithfulness of which they themselves may be unaware. Their service to their neighbors is service to God. The good they do helps build the Kingdom no less than the good done by Christians builds that same Kingdom. And, they challenge us Christians to deeper fidelity to the Gospel.

Does this mean, then, that there is no reason for "our company," the Church, to exist? Is it wrong for us to continue to invite others to join the community of those who proclaim Christ, who worship the Father through Christ in the Holy Spirit?

No. Jesus himself called men and women into that "company." We companions of Jesus have an essential vocation. All men and women are called to live in the dignity of children of God. All men and women have a right to know that dignity and a right to rejoice in it and give thanks for it. They are entitled to the support and guidance that the "company" can give in fulfilling the will of God for the world.

Our "company" lives in the world as a sign of the Reign of God. That Reign is bigger than our company. It includes men and women of all times and climes. Most of those people have not been, and will not be, part of the "company." We rejoice that even so, they are part of that Kingdom.

Twenty-Seventh Sunday of the Year (B)

Evidence for the basic accuracy of the Gospel accounts of the resurrection is the fact that the testimony is given by women. That is not because women are more trustworthy than men. It is simply that unless it were absolutely true, the men who wrote the Gospels would never have said so. Saying so damaged their case.

In the society in which Jesus and his disciples lived, women were not allowed to give testimony as equals of men. So, legally speaking, the Church had no basis for believing in the resurrection. The witnesses were not qualified to give testimony.

The example of divorce in Mark's Gospel is another case of women being treated differently from men. A husband could abuse his wife, deprive her and use her but she had no means of escape. A woman did not have the ability to divorce her husband. (Mark's mention of a woman divorcing is something he added to the words of Jesus out of his own Gentile background; Jewish women could not divorce their husbands.) The right of divorce belonged to the man, and no legal proceedings were required. A woman could be made homeless and deprived of her children and all support on the whim of her husband. One rabbi taught that a burnt meal was sufficient grounds for divorce.

There was another group in the time of Jesus that lacked basic rights: children. Children were possessions. In Roman law, a father who killed his child faced no legal penalty.

Children are still abused by adults throughout the world. They labor in dangerous conditions. They are forced into sexual slavery. They are provided with "entertainment" that poisons their minds and spirits. They are aborted, deprived of education, forced to live in inhuman conditions, victimized by war and poverty, and physically and emotionally abused.

Jesus defended two groups in his society that had no defense. He forbade discarding wives or denying children their right to a place among his followers.

There is no toleration in the Reign of God for the bias that infected his society and infects our own.

People who differ from some social or personal norm in race, nationality, social class, religion, age, physical abilities, education, sexual orientation, language, tastes, employment (or lack of it) or just about anything else are frequently ignored, deprived and even abused.

Women and children still experience this. Others include refugees and migrants, persons with AIDS, the disabled and racial, ethnic and religious minorities.

The Reign of God is as big as eternity, but it has no room for discrimination.

Discrimination is a terrible sin because it denies creation. The truth that God made the world in love is not threatened by science. It is denied by those who treat others as if they were not children of God's loving creation. Jesus was angry when he saw his disciples discriminate. Dare we assume that his anger is any less when we do it?

What are we to do? The first step in conversion is to recognize our sinfulness. I must examine my life and attitudes. I must pay attention when I meet, see or hear about someone different from myself. Do I judge others by criteria other than their being sons and daughters of God?

Following the admission of sin, there is contrition. I must pray for a heart that is pained by my sin. Then, there is confession. This is true in the sacrament (have I ever thought to confess my bias?) and in my day-to-day life. I must confess to others and myself that I am capable of discrimination, that I fall into the sin. Confession to myself is important because it is the source of amendment.

I must pray for courage to turn from sin, to cooperate with God's call to change my life. That is not easy when the sin is one I may have inherited from my community, family or society. Finally, there is penance, action to heal the damage caused by sin. I must act to bring an end to anything that denies the children of God their full dignity.

To do less is to decide that God's Reign should exclude certain people. Perhaps it can. But, in that case, we may find that the ones who are excluded are we.

Twenty-Eighth Sunday of the Year (B)

There is a guru in almost every area of human interest, offering enlightenment to those who want it. Even the life of the spirit is not exempt from the pursuit of self-improvement. Books purporting to give easy enlightenment for only the cost of a volume fill the shelves. Most of them are simple-minded; some are downright harmful.

There is a paradox in our age's pursuit of self-improvement. We are looking for easy success. If I read the right book, find the right physical or psychic trainer, attend the right seminar, watch the right video or meet the right person, I will be enlightened.

I need not make too much effort myself — the reading or the encounter should suffice. Lots of people watch exercise videos instead of taking a walk.

And yet, I am not totally irresponsible. I really want to improve myself. I really want to be perfectly fit physically, emotionally, spiritually, socially and financially. I just want it to happen instantly, with a minimum of effort. I want to improve my life, but preferably without changing it.

The man who ran up to Jesus may have jogged out of our own time. He wanted to improve himself. "Good teacher, what must I do to share in everlasting life?"

Perhaps Jesus had been recommended by whatever was the first-century equivalent of daytime television. So, possibly to reassure himself that he had really found the right guru, he called Jesus "good." Jesus told him not to overdo it, to keep a sense of perspective. "Why do you call me good? No one is good but God alone."

Then, Jesus told the man the way to live perfectly, the commandments of God. Now, the man was very earnest, so he could honestly say, "Teacher, I have observed all these since my childhood."

So, the Lord gave him a bit more advice, the absolutely foolproof way the man thought he was looking for. "There is one thing more you must do."

The man's eyes went wide, his head moved forward so that he would not miss a word of wisdom. "Go and sell what you have and give to the poor; you will then have treasure in heaven. After that, come and follow me."

"At these words, the man's face fell."

The man earnestly sought the answer. So, Jesus gave it to him, inviting him to live without assurance, without guarantees. He told the man to give up all that he depended upon and start wandering the road to who-knows-where.

That was more than the man was willing to do.

The difficulty was that he wanted assurances. He called Jesus "good" in order to assure himself he had made the right choice. However, the world offers no guarantees. Jesus challenged him to live in the real world, to give up all that might allow him to avoid the truth that there is no easy way to share in everlasting life. (And everlasting life is what we all really want; all our other searches are symptoms of that desire.)

So, the man went off, probably in search of someone who would give him more palatable advice.

I, too, earnestly desire everlasting life. I, too, fear living the kind of life that leads to it. I am like the disciples who "were completely overwhelmed at this and exclaimed to one another, 'Then who can be saved?'"

No matter how earnestly I desire it, I cannot bring myself to do what is necessary to achieve salvation. "For mortals it is impossible, but not for God; for God all things are possible." God will provide what I need. I must be willing to accept what I am offered. The man in today's Gospel could not. Can I?

Twenty-Ninth Sunday of the Year (B)

The Gospel challenges the world's values and its sinfulness. Few of us have any problem believing that. Our problem comes when we are reminded that the Gospel also challenges the Church's values and sinfulness.

The values of the Church are not solely the values of the Reign of God. They cannot be. After all, the Church is people like you and me Much of my life is conducted without reference to Jesus. I look for the easy way out. I avoid situations where I might have to make my faith clear to others. I postpone the prayer, study and action I know I should do.

Add to me all the other Christians who have ever lived, and the sinfulness and weakness of the Church should not surprise us. The wonder is that the Holy Spirit is able to work through such a weak community.

James and John were fishermen who left their father, their boat and their nets to follow Jesus. In spite of the fact that they had seen his deeds and heard his teaching, they ask for special treatment. The other apostles are indignant at this. Their indignation, however, is not because James and John have asked for high places, but because they want those places for themselves.

In Mark's Gospel, those with a special role in the community, the Twelve, are the prime example of people seeking a special place. We can see the same situation today. Have you ever been to a Church function at which special places had not been set aside for clergy and Religious? Usually, it is others who have to search for places on their own.

When it comes to titles and forms of address, we do no better. We set up all sorts of distinctions, primarily among those publicly committed to being servants. Our bishops wear headgear probably derived from that of Roman emperors. H.L. Mencken defined an archbishop as "a Christian ecclesiastic of a rank superior to that attained by Christ."

Some of our clergy are addressed as "monsignor" ("my lord"). The "servant of the servants of God" is addressed by his supposed masters as "Your Holiness." Even "Brother," "Father" and "Sister" become titles of rank and entitlement rather than of service.

This does not mean that popes are incapable of holiness, or that priests cannot be true fathers in faith or that Brothers and Sisters never walk with us on our journey. It does mean, however, that over time we have come to invest a lot — perhaps too much — in titles and status.

The temptation to status is not limited to one group in the Church, and no one is exempt. Each of us is tempted to want recognition for what we do, say, or think. It is natural.

Sometimes, being a Christian means going against doing what comes naturally. The whole world does what comes naturally, and that is why it needs salvation. Jesus requires that his followers live the reverse of what the world deems natural, that we be signs of that salvation.

Therefore, he tells the disciples that we must be slaves. We should be concerned with service rather than an egotistical pursuit of status, position or recognition.

Jesus himself is, of course, the prime example of this. He experienced our weakness and temptation. The difference is that he did not yield to them. He remained a servant to all.

Today, he warns us against a real danger to the fulfilment of our mission, the temptation to status, prestige and recognition. He reminds us that his way is the way of the Cross. His followers can expect only that as reward for their faithfulness to him.

Thirtieth Sunday of the Year (B)

Until Bartimaeus cries, "Jesus, Son of David, have pity on me!" the only others in Mark's Gospel who have called Jesus by any title that recognizes him as Messiah have been demons. Even the men and women who have journeyed with Jesus have not seen clearly enough to realize who he is.

The Gospels do not hesitate to put us followers of Jesus in a bad light. We, represented by the disciples, can be so dense that we miss something that evil demons know and that even a blind man can see. That is, that Jesus is the presence of the Reign of God among us.

Bartimaeus cries out without fear, unlike the demons. Instead, he cries out in hope and faith. Perhaps until the time comes that we really need him, we will never see him as he really is.

Sitting on the side of the road, hoping for some charity that would help him stay alive, Bartimaeus knew he needed help. Real help. His concerns were worth bringing to the Lord.

When Bartimaeus throws off his cloak and jumps up to meet Jesus, the Lord asks him a simple question: "What do you want me to do for you?" It's the same question we heard him ask James and John last week. They gave the wrong answer. They asked for prestige, something no one really needs.

Bartimaeus gives the right answer: "I want to see." That's something we all need, to really see. But, what is it we must see?

Strangely enough, I am blind about my needs. I think there are many things I need, but do I really need them? Or, do I need them as much as I think I do?

Jesus offers something that cannot be seen with eyes blinded by the offerings and enticements of this world. He offers the Reign of God.

There are times in my life when I realize my true need. Usually, such times come when I am fearful or in pain. Death is an obvious eye opener. So are the "cousins of death," the events that threaten what we think we need in this life. When we must face their loss, we realize how much we need the power of God. Then, we can cry out to Jesus, "Son of David, Savior, have pity on me!" We finally see as well as Bartimaeus.

Then, an interesting thing happens. When Bartimaeus, after having declared who Jesus really is, asks to be given his sight, Jesus does nothing. He merely declares that Bartimaeus's faith has healed him already. The blind man's saying he wanted to see was all it took for him to really see. When he called Jesus "Son of David," he was already seeing. The healing of his eyes was a symbol of the true sight, the true insight, that Bartimaeus already possessed.

That is very comforting to me, truly Good News. It is enough for me to turn to the Lord and call out in my pain, confusion and doubt. I do not need great understanding or even a faith that is alive and lively at all times. I can spend my life at the side of the road, wondering and hoping. As soon as I call, the Lord is there with me.

Bartimaeus has an interesting response to his healing. He apparently disobeys the Lord. Jesus tells him, "Be on your way!" Instead, Mark tells us, "Immediately he received his sight and started to follow him up the road." From now on, the way of Jesus is also the way of Bartimaeus.

Once he has recognized Jesus, once we have recognized Jesus, the only way is his way. We follow him to the cross and beyond to everlasting life.

Thirty-First Sunday of the Year (B)

The Jewish day begins at sundown, a custom the Church follows to some extent. For example, Sunday and major feasts start the evening before. That is the reason Catholics celebrate Sunday Mass on Saturday evening. In fact, there is no Saturday evening prayer or night prayer. Instead, we pray the first of two sets of Sunday evening and night prayers.

The reading in the first of those night prayers begins: "Hear, O Israel! The Lord is our God, the Lord alone. You shall love the Lord your God with all your heart, and with all your soul, and with all your might."

So, the first day of our week begins with "the first of all the commandments." It is not only that, however, it is the basic Jewish declaration of faith. Just as Christians can sum up their faith in the phrase "Jesus Christ is Lord," Jews use these words to declare what they believe. So, it was natural that Jesus would cite them as the prime commandment. From childhood he had recited them daily. After all, he was a Jew.

That should be obvious to his followers. And yet, at many times throughout history followers of a Jew named Jesus have attacked his people. And our failures are not limited to the way we have treated Jews. We haven't treated each other any better. In fact, looking at the way I treat people around me would not be a good advertisement for Christianity. What has gone wrong in our lives?

The way to find out where I have gone wrong is to look at the commandments. And if I want to find the most basic wrong in my life, I should look to the most basic commandment.

The problem with the first commandment is that little word "all." I'm willing to love God in a half-hearted way. Church on Sunday and occasional prayers are fine. But, loving God with all my heart, all my soul, all my mind and all my strength? That doesn't leave much for me.

When I carry a grudge, it is with me all the time. Someone in love carries thoughts of the beloved around all the time. But what about my thoughts of God? The commandment says "Keep these words that I am commanding you today in your heart."

The fact is, I can go for days without giving God a single thought. Oh, I might think from time to time about religious duties and such. But of God? Even when I am in church, I seldom think of God.

Since I seldom think of God, I don't keep the first commandment. Because I don't keep the first commandment, I fall short in keeping the second. Being a Christian is not about behaving toward others in a certain way. It is about having a special kind of relationship with God. All else follows from that.

How can I grow in that relationship? One way is to do what I do to build any relationship. Talk. Carry on a conversation with God. I shouldn't bother calling it "prayer." That makes it seem too like a task or too exalted. Just talk. I should do it all day long, or at least when I remember to. I should say anything, even if it's just, "God, I'm going to feed the goldfish now."

Such an on-going conversation with God could gradually lead me to keeping love of God in my heart, soul, mind and strength. Then, I would be able to love my neighbor as God does.

Thirty-Second Sunday of the Year (B)

For most of us, I think our treasure is not measured with coin counting machines, but with clocks. Time is our treasure.

We add one day to the calendar every four years, but some of us feel that we should add an extra hour or two to each day. We are busy. There never seems to be enough time to do all we have to do, let alone all we want to do. We try to do several things at once, "multi-tasking."

Not only do I not have enough time, I have less and less of it every moment. I am running out of time. Sooner or later, I will have no more time. Each second brings me one second closer to the end.

Yes, indeed, time is a treasure for me. I have a limited amount of it, and I don't even know how little. I have a lifetime of duties and desires to fit into that rare time, yet it disappears even faster than a poor widow's savings.

Two thousand years ago, Jesus sat opposite the temple treasury to watch people being generous. Today, he might sit across the street from one of those big digital clocks that record the passing tenths of seconds in a blur.

For, if I wish to imitate the widow's generosity today, I would not give a few coins or even a big bundle of bills. I would give time.

There is no shortage of uses to which my time could be put. There are lonely people who need someone who will give time to listen to their stories, to join them on strolls, to run errands for them. There are children who need the time of adults in order to learn, to make their dreams come true. These lonely people, these children, may even be in our own homes. Projects and programs to make our world better need the time of talented men and women.

All of that is obvious. Frankly, though, it is easier for me to give money. I do not have the time to spare. However, the widow in the Gospel did not have any money to spare, yet that did not stop her from giving it. How could she do that? After all, she needed those two coins in order to live. How could she do with her money treasure what I find so hard to do with my time treasure?

There are two answers: trust and gratitude. The woman was able to give all that she had because she trusted God. She knew that ultimately all that she had came from God and that no matter what she gave up, nothing would separate her from God's love. She might starve because of her generosity, but God's life-giving love would still embrace her.

This is very different from the scribes against whom Jesus speaks at the start of the Gospel passage, those bigwigs "who like to parade around in their robes and accept marks of respect in public, front seats in the synagogues, and places of honor at banquets." They are not willing to trust in God, to trust that in time they would be rewarded. They prefer to seek instant recognition from others now rather than from God later. With that attitude, they cannot risk their treasure, because what they have now is all they expect to have.

The woman knew better. She knew that what she had, her treasure of two coins, was nothing compared to what God offers. So, in gratitude she could give them up.

God offers me eternity. Can I, in gratitude, find ways to offer up my treasure of time?

Thirty-Third Sunday of the Year (B)

I once lived in a house that had a fig tree outside it. It never bore fruit. It certainly never gave me insights into God's Reign. This week's passage from Mark seems like that fig tree. It does not bear fruit. As one scholar wrote about the details of the passage: "it is not easy to assess either the meaning they had for first-century Christians or the meaning that modern Christians are to draw from them."

Yet, the first-century Christian who wrote this Gospel felt there was some meaning to be drawn from the passage as a whole, if not from the details. Ever since, the Church has continued to proclaim it, even though the details are either wrong or incomprehensible. Is there some meaning in this passage for our age as well?

In our lives there are events and situations that to us, at least, seem as overwhelmingly terrible as the sun dying or the stars falling. My plans and dreams fail. A relationship is betrayed. One I love suffers. I will die. Natural and man-made disasters destroy livelihoods and lives. War, injustice, violence, corruption and poverty seem too powerful to be driven from our world. When these things strike home with me, the world may carry on, but so far as I am concerned, it may as well have ended.

Situations like that are invitations to despair. Why should I carry on? Why trust in God's love? Why risk loving or forgiving? A sort of spiritual and emotional paralysis can set in. I cease to desire, cease to pray, cease to hope. I may wish I were dead and gone. I may even be tempted to make that happen. The end of a world — whether it be the planet we live on, a society or nation, or my own private world — is a terrible thing.

Is there an alternative to despair? There is hope, of course, but how can I hope when my world is destroyed? Whether another tells me to "cheer up," or I say it to myself, I cannot do it. "Cheer up" is useful advice for small disappointments, but it does not work when a world ends. I want something upon which I can either restore my world or build a new one.

Jesus tells us to learn from the way that seemingly dead trees send forth new shoots. There is something about the world God made that refuses to die forever. The flowing sap and tiny buds remind us that we may have to look hard to see signs of new life, but they are there.

Does that mean that after a bit of time I can expect my world to be reborn as it was, as I want it? Painful experience says "No!" The fig tree is only a parable, not a paradigm or model.

So, what, then, is the evidence that can draw me from the edge of despair? Parables are nice, but my life is not a parable. It is real.

The most conclusive evidence is in something else that Jesus says. In the midst of destruction, the Son of Man comes. When he comes, "he will send out the angels, and gather his elect from the four winds, from the ends of the earth to the ends of heaven."

The risen Lord, the one who has gone through death to life, the conqueror of destruction, is with us when our world is destroyed. He does not reverse the destruction. Instead, his calling us to join him is compensation for all that we must endure. I may not think so, but I must at least have enough trust in the Lord to believe that he, having experienced the end of his world on the cross, knows better than I.

The Good News is not that God will make everything work out as we wish but that he is with us in a special way when it seems our world is ending.

Thirty-Fourth Sunday of the Year
Christia the King (B)

Since the American and French revolutions of the eighteenth century, the number of countries with kings and queens has been shrinking. The number of countries where royalty actually rules has shrunk even faster.

Since kings and queens are becoming the stuff of fairy tales and legends, why celebrate a feast declaring Christ to be a king? Certainly Jesus was not a king. He had nothing to do with ruling anyone or anything.

Ironically, this feast was introduced long after kingship's decline began. It is surprisingly new. It is also surprisingly subversive of the way we use power in this world. It is very relevant.

The feast of Christ the King was introduced by Pope Pius XI in 1925, partly in response to the growth of totalitarian and super-nationalistic governments in Europe. Under those governments, dictators claimed and attempted to exercise absolute authority over the thoughts and actions of people. The state, embodied in the ruler or ruling party, was supreme. The duty of citizens was to serve the state. Such ideologies still rule huge portions of the world's people.

In the face of this, the Church declared that the only true ruler of people's minds and hearts is Christ. No earthly power can usurp his authority. No earthly power can treat men and women as tools of power or as "resources" to be used and abused at the whim of governments or others. Today is the feast of human rights.

It is easy to point out examples in the political realm where individuals are trampled so that others may usurp God's rule over creation. But, it is not just politicians who must recognize that Christ is King.

Where else can we see situations in which the powerful "lord it over" others? Where else are people used by their "masters" and made to serve ends that are not appropriate to men and women who are children of God?

Certainly the business world falls into the trap. Some enterprises even talk openly about "human resource management" as if people were merely assets like machinery or a pile of coal. There are obviously degrading situations of child labor, indentured labor (a fancy name for slavery), the sex trade and labor in health- and life-threatening conditions. But, men and women who sit at desks and make international phone calls can also be treated as if their sole value were in their usefulness to a corporation and its aims.

Even families are challenged by today's feast. We may not even have to leave our own homes to see families that suffer under the dominance of an absolute monarch who may masquerade as a father, a mother, an aunt, an uncle or even a child.

Even the Church is not immune. Some studies have shown that the basic reason men and women leave priesthood or religious life is the abuse of power by "religious superiors."

Today the Church says, "No!" to all such tyrannies. There is only One who has any claim to absolute obedience. That one is Christ. Anyone else who claims such power is a usurper.

Why is that? Isn't it enough to grant that Christ is king in heaven? Isn't his claim to rule on earth "meddling in internal affairs"? However, in the Incarnation Christ has become a citizen of the world. For this king, there are no foreign relations.

We are images and heirs of God. We are the princes and princesses of Christ the King. Each of us without exception has a dignity that cannot be subordinated to any person, ideology or worldly desire.

Today we say that Christ is King. He is not merely King of Heaven; he is King of the Universe, including you and me. When we say Christ is King, we say we belong to him and to no others. We cannot, then, be used or abused, since that is an attack upon his subjects and his sovereignty.

First Sunday of Lent, (B)

Whether it be giving up sweets for Lent, giving up marriage for life, giving up chances at wealth to serve others, or whatever else, Christian asceticism does not arise from a belief that the pleasures of life are evil or that we must punish ourselves for our sins. Neither is it religious athleticism, an attempt to turn ourselves into spiritual superheroes who earn, deserve or wrest God's grace.

Asceticism is an act of faith, a chance to remind ourselves and proclaim to others that we need fear no loss so long as we are embraced by God's love. In a sense, it is a preparation for death, when we give up everything except the undying love of God.

During Lent, we "give up" various things. Kids give up sweets, adults give up alcohol or meals. Some individuals and families engage in what may be the most drastic form of modern self-abnegation, putting aside various electronic devices from Ash Wednesday until Easter.

What happens when I give something up? Well, the first thing is that I notice it's missing. My stomach rumbles, my eyes stare at a blank screen. I go through withdrawal. If I don't panic and give in right away, pouring a drink, opening a bag of snacks and grabbing for some electronic device or the TV remote, I realize a few things.

The first is that my life has depended upon things that are not actually essential. After all, I'm not dying of my Lenten practice. I can live without.

The second is that by voluntarily doing without I understand a bit of what many of my brothers and sisters must experience and endure every day. I feel communion with the rest of the world.

Third, I realize I'm turning a profit. Each day I do without something, I reduce my expenditures. I can lose weight and make money by doing nothing! I also turn a profit of time. Time I spent on what I've given up is now available for new things. I may decide to use those profits for the sake of others.

Fourth, I am reminded that I can indeed "do without" because no matter what I lose, God is with me. I can go hungry, I can even starve. I will die. But, nothing can separate me from the love of God. And so, I pray in gratitude, in awe, in hope. My growling stomach can be a call to prayer.

Ultimately, our Lenten practices are an opportunity to renew faith in God's love that went to the Cross for us and showed that the love of God is stronger than evil, stronger than death.

But why now? Why spend our penitential 40 days before the Sacred Triduum of Holy Thursday, Good Friday and the Easter Vigil instead of, for instance, before Christmas or Pentecost?

It's tied to something very important that happens at the Easter Vigil and at Mass on Easter Sunday. The Easter Vigil is when catechumens are baptized. Lent was originally the season of their preparation. At Easter, those of us who are already baptized renew our own baptismal commitment.

Because it is primarily a time for catechumens, Lent is a time for the Church to prepare to welcome them. Are we worthy to lead these men and women to Christ? Are we dedicated enough to encourage them on the way? Are we examples to them of what their new life in Christ will mean? Lent is a time for our conversion.

Mark's Gospel gives us a summary of Jesus' message: "This is the time of fulfillment. The reign of God is at hand! Reform your lives and believe in the good news." The Lord has come among us, and God is with us. Easter, with its promise that life is unconquered by suffering and death and in fact comes through them, is near.

The Lord calls us to a change of life, a change we exercise in some small way in Lent as a means of recommitting ourselves at Easter to the big reform we accepted in our baptismal commitment.

That reform is a life free from enslavement to the things around me, free of the need to find my value in the things I own or use. It is sharing my time, talents and treasures with my brothers and sisters. It is joyful, grateful hope that in my death I am not lost to God. In other words, it is Lent.

Second Sunday of Lent (B)

One evening at a parish Bible group's discussion of Abraham's willingness to sacrifice his son Isaac, the first few speakers were nuns who lived in the parish.

Each made observations about how Abraham's faith challenges us to deeper trust in God. They spoke of how Abraham's example called them to recognize their attachment to things of this world.

When the last sister had spoken, Mr. M's turn came to give his reflections. I always envied his ability to get to the heart of a passage of Scripture without intellectualizing it or making it so abstract that it sounded uncomfortably like some of the worst homilies I had ever preached.

"Maybe I'm a bad Christian, but I'll tell you right now: I don't care if God himself told me to do it, there's no way I'd ever hurt a hair of my boy's head, let alone be willing to kill him! If God wants that, I don't want God!"

The issue of child sacrifice was not an abstraction for Mr. M. He had a son and a daughter whom he loved no less than Abraham loved Isaac. Mr. M knew what Abraham had to face in order to obey God.

How often when I hear the readings at Mass, or when I read the Bible or pray words of Scripture do I look upon them as beautiful phrases, as food for thought, as points for reflection? Most of the time. Sometimes, the words seem merely ants crawling across a page or bees droning in the sanctuary.

How often do I allow the Word of God to be a real message addressed to me, comforting me, challenging me, calling me? Oh, I like to think I do. Like the sisters that evening or like me had I not been able to swallow my words while still unsaid, I can make reflections upon the Word. But they come from my head. The Word doesn't get mixed up in my real day-to-day thoughts, emotions and activities.

Lent is a special time to hear the word of God. Lenten practices, including, perhaps, a renewed familiarity with Scripture, free me to some extent from what distracts me from attending to the Lord. During Lent, I can grow to be more like Mr. M, ready to not merely hear the Word of God, but to hear it as something addressed to me here and now.

In today's Gospel passage, three disciples hear the Word of God addressed to them. The voice from heaven confirms the vocation of Jesus announced at his Baptism: "This is my Son, my beloved."

The voice spoke at the beginning of Jesus' ministry. Now, as that ministry reaches its culmination, the glory that will be Christ's through the Cross is shown to the disciples. The baptismal call to start off on the road to the Cross is the same as the proclamation of Jesus in glory.

It may seem strange that early in Lent, a season we tend to see as gloomy, we are presented with a picture of the Lord in glory. However, if we look at the Transfiguration with the sort of heart that Mr. M had, we may find it appropriate, comforting and encouraging for ourselves.

The Transfiguration is not just a story about Jesus on a mountain once upon a time in a land far away. It is my story. As I prepare to renew my baptismal commitment at Easter, I remember that at my own Baptism, God said, "This is my beloved child."

God loves me as Abraham loved Isaac, or as Mr. M loved his son. In fact, as St. Paul reminds me in the second reading, God went so far as to actually sacrifice the Son for me. "Is it possible that he who did not spare his own Son but handed him over for the sake of us all will not grant us all things besides?"

Today's Gospel is a Lenten reminder that the gift of being a beloved child of God that I received in Baptism leads to my own transfiguration. I walk the way of the Cross in this world, but it is a way that leads to incomparable glory.

Sometimes, the word of God can be a threatening challenge. Today, it is "tidings of comfort and joy." Let's hear these words like Abraham and Mr. M, ready to hear the word of God as personally addressed to me, to us.

Third Sunday of Lent (B)

Jesus swung a whip at sheep and oxen that would soon be sacrificed, terrorizing them a bit more before they faced the knife. He attacked people making a living by providing a service to worshippers who needed animals to sacrifice. Dove sellers served the poor who could not afford bigger sacrifices. The commandment against graven images meant that people who wanted to contribute to the temple had to change coins bearing images of pagan gods or rulers into temple money. So, why does Jesus go after them in a way so alien to our view of "gentle Jesus, meek and mild"?

The layout of the temple tells us. There were sections of the temple for different people. The high priest could go where no one else could, into the Holy of Holies. There were sections for priests and Levites, for men, for women. The outermost courtyard was open to non-Jews who wished to associate themselves with the prayers and sacrifices going on in the temple. It was here that the needs of those entering the temple for worship were met.

Imagine yourself as a gentile coming to the temple to pray. You know you're not allowed inside, but you're willing to settle for any place that allows you to be close to the temple of God. You climb the steps to the courtyard reserved for you, and what do you find?

The courtyard is full of cattle, tables and crowds carrying on business. There's no room for you! The needs of temple worshipers have crowded you out from being a worshiper yourself.

That is the source of the Lord's anger. All people have the right to come to God, but the religiosity of some was blocking others. So, Jesus drove out those who had usurped the prayer place of the outsiders. His problem was not with the temple, but with the fact that the very temple of God had somehow become an obstacle to men and women who were seeking God.

One reason we read this passage in Lent is that the attack on the vendors and money changers was one of the reasons that leaders in Jerusalem brought about Jesus' death. As we draw closer to our commemoration of the death of Jesus, we trace some of his steps to the Cross.

However, there is another reason to reflect upon this event during the season of repentance and conversion. The situation that enraged Jesus continues.

There are no animal vendors in our churches, and any parish struggling to pay expenses will accept contributions no matter whose picture is on them. However, we, like the temple vendors, block men and women who seek God.

Imagine once again that you are that non-believer hoping to draw closer to God. You look at those who claim to show the presence of God in the world. What do you see?

One thing is a history of Christians killing, exploiting and abusing each other and the rest of the world. You turn to the news, and see injustice and violence in the part of the world with the longest, most sustained Christian presence. You see the Church divided into denominations and sects, considering what may or may not have been said centuries ago more important than a shared vocation to be a sign of God's unifying love.

Somehow you find your way through those obstacles, and encounter an actual community of Christians.

You find yourself in a mob of people who neither know nor care about the so-called brothers or sisters worshiping with them. You see worship that leaves you wondering if God, the creator of beauty, could have anything to do with something so dead.

In sadness, you turn away, because Christians have blocked your meeting God just as the temple vendors blocked the Gentiles' access to their place of prayer.

Mid-way to our celebration of the Cross and Easter, we reflect on how we are like the animals, tables and vendors in the temple, interfering with others' finding the Lord. As individuals and as a community, we must repent. But we are called to more than guilt feelings.

Lent is a time to commit myself to living in such a way that a world looking for God will find in me and the Church a welcome, an example and a guide.

Considering how Christ dealt with those who interfered with others' search for God in the temple, I dare not fail to purge from my life or from our community anything that may provoke his anger at me.

Fourth Sunday of Lent (B)

The heart of what Christians celebrate and proclaim is a verse from John that deserves memorization and frequent recitation and meditation: "God so loved the world that he gave his only Son, so that everyone who believes in him may not perish but may have eternal life."

What is the world that God so loved? Is it an ideal place where everyone lives in justice and peace? Is it an Eden where sin is absent and humankind lives in harmony with itself and nature? God would certainly love such a world, but unfortunately it doesn't exist.

Does God love the good things that happen in our world? Justice and peace really do occur. God's beautiful creation is appreciated, is protected and has its harmful effects softened or prevented. This is a world where love among peoples and worship of God actually happen. Perhaps God so loves the good things about our world as to send the Son as a reward to those responsible for that goodness.

However, that is not what the passage says. It says "the world" without modification. The world God loves is this world, the one in which we actually spend our lives. It is a world of injustice and discord as well as of love and cooperation. It is a world where there seems to never be good unmarred by pain, stupidity, selfishness, weakness, hatred, sin and death. The good news is that God loves the world as it is, not as it could be or should be.

What makes this good news is the fact that we are part of that world so loved by God. We do not have to earn God's love. We have it, bad as we can be, to the extent of God's sending the Son to save us from whatever keeps us from experiencing that love in its fulness.

Does this seem a strange message for Lent, a season to reflect upon repentance and our need for salvation? Shouldn't we be gloomy in order to set off the joy of Easter? Isn't it a few weeks too early to be hearing such incredibly good news?

Later in the passage, there seems to be an opening for a bit of gloom: "Whoever does not believe is already condemned for not believing in the name of God's only Son." Does this mean that we are saved by believing in a single word and damned for not believing in it? Are all those who do not know the word "Jesus" doomed?

A pitfall for those who look to Scripture (and other Church teachings) for knowledge of God is what theologians call "objectification." It is the tendency to treat the words of Scripture as if they were a checklist rather like instructions for flying a plane or baking a cake. However, they are more like poetry and should be read that way.

In the Bible, one's name is the equivalent of one's self. To believe in the name of Jesus is not to make declarations regarding how the neighbors called him; it is to accept what he really is, perhaps without ever hearing the word "Jesus" (the condition of most men and women alive today).

What is he, then? That brings us back to the overall theme of his words to Nicodemus. He is the love of God made present among us. He is the source of eternal life, offered to the whole world because God loves the whole world. To accept his name is to live in the love of God, not refusing any of the gifts God offers us, whether we know the donor or not.

Lent is the season when we prepare to renew our baptismal commitment in solidarity with those being baptized at Easter. It is a time of preparation to re-dedicate ourselves to proclaiming to the world the good news that God indeed loves us now, here, as we really are.

God's love will not wait or depend upon my repentance. That love will not make any demand upon me except that I accept it. That love will not even be overcome by my death, and so is the source of eternal life.

Can I really believe that? I can easily believe that I must repent, but it's harder for me to believe that God loves me whether or not I do anything to earn it. God loves me not as I could be or should be, but as I am. Even I don't do that.

Fifth Sunday of Lent (B)

When Jesus speaks in John's Gospel, he often makes it easy to misunderstand him. Nicodemus, for example, gets mocked by Jesus for having difficulty figuring out how a grown man can be born again. Today Jesus does it again, saying one thing, but meaning more than folks would catch at first hearing.

When Jesus says he will be lifted up, the expectation is that he is describing some sort of glorification. "I — once I am lifted up from the earth — will draw all to myself." After all, the passage begins with his declaration that "the hour has come for the Son of Man to be glorified." It sounds encouraging. Jesus will be lifted up from this earth to something better and we will be drawn to him there. Good news, but the wrong message.

John "lets the beans out of the bag" by telling us that Jesus is actually talking about the way he will die, lifted up from the earth on a cross. Do I really want to be drawn to him there?

The paradox is that both understandings of what Jesus says are correct. For John, the Crucifixion is the glorification of Christ and his glorification is inseparable from the Cross. How can that be? How can death by torture be glory?

As we approach Holy Week, it is time to think about the puzzle of John's equating death and glory. Theoretically, Jesus could have saved us by doing something other than dying. Sharing intellectual or spiritual enlightenment would have been easier for us to handle.

Let's start by thinking about glory. We may not be sure what it is, but (aside from John's equating it with the Cross), we think that, on the whole, it's more pleasant than being tortured.

It's hard to describe glory, since we have not experienced it fully. However, we have all had moments that have seemed close enough to the real thing to give us a hint of what glory is. Over the centuries, we have used light, halos, trumpets, anthems, dances and ecstasies to describe it. To put it prosaically, glory is the experience of being embraced by God's overwhelming love.

That love has no limit. Time, sin and death cannot overcome it. It is a love by which God gives life in all its richness. When I intuit it or like a contemplative experience it directly, I am transformed, transported by a joy so great it can feel like pain.

But, can I trust it? How can I be sure of it? After all, I will die. Even before that happens, I feel the love of God less often and less intensely than I feel its seeming absence. Believing in it doesn't make my life any easier. It certainly doesn't make me a nicer person. So, is the love of God that the Church proclaims real?

This is where John's insight that the Cross is the glorification of Christ gives comforting assurance. Even in his death that seemed as far as possible from the love of God or anyone else, Jesus was in glory because he was embraced by God's love and showing the nature of God's love.

God's is a crucified love. It is so completely self-giving as to be a self-immolation, the death of God. In John's account of the Last Supper, Jesus says there is no greater love than to lay down one's life for one's friends. On the Cross, that is what God does. The eternal God dies of love.

The ultimate example of the presence of God's love, the ultimate glory, is indeed the Cross. So, Jesus can say that in being lifted up on the Cross he will draw all to himself in glory.

And what of us? At Easter, we will renew our baptismal union with the death of Christ. Jesus says that unless a grain of wheat fall to the earth and die, it remains merely a grain. I will certainly die. In various ways, I have suffered and will suffer. Can I believe that even in these experiences, I am embraced by the love of God, that I am in glory?

That is one of the things Lenten practices should be teaching me in a low-key way. In deprivation, privation, suffering and death I am embraced by God. In those experiences I am, in fact, most closely embraced by God, because they are the times I can myself be most like God whose love is a suffering love.

Passion or Palm Sunday (B)

Is God some kind of monster?

Before you say "NO!" too quickly, think about what we commemorate and even celebrate this week, the torture to death of Jesus. We say that the death by crucifixion of Jesus, the Son of God, was in accord with the will of God the Father.

Doesn't that sound like some form of child abuse? What kind of father would expect such a death of his child? And what kind of people are we who celebrate it? Let's face it, it all looks rather ghoulish at first glance.

We might try to avoid the issue by saying that the crucifixion of Jesus was some sort of accident that was not part of God's plan. Or, that it was the inevitable result of Jesus' confrontation with the religious and political authorities of his day.

But the New Testament does not let us use those sorts of comforting evasions. The entire message of the Scriptures is that in going to the Cross, Jesus was fulfilling the Father's will. His whole life was a way of the cross to Calvary. Jesus is not the good teacher and healer who was murdered; he is the crucified one who taught and healed. That is the reason the Cross is the symbol of Christianity. Ours is the religion of the Cross.

But why? Why do we say that the death of Jesus rather than, for example, his healing the sick is the source of salvation? Wasn't the Incarnation, the coming of God the Son among us as one of us, enough? What is the link between his death and our liberation from sin?

Perhaps the place to begin thinking about it is to see if there might be some sort of link between death and sin. We often say that death is a result of sin, a punishment for the basic estrangement we have from God, each other and our true self that we call Original Sin.

But, what if it were the other way around? What if sin were a result of death? Clearly, death is a part of life. All living beings die, even those that do not sin. Death is built into creation. It is the engine that drives evolution, with species and individuals dying to make room for yet others.

However, most of creation does not know that it will die. A few animals seem to have some idea of death, but none besides ourselves seem to understand that death is not just something "out there." For us humans, death is very "up close and personal." In fact, it is something that will happen to me one day. And I know it.

The engagingly lively dead in Tim Burton's film, *The Corpse Bride* sing: "Die, die, we all pass away/But don't wear a frown/Because it's really okay/You might try and hide/And you might try and pray/But we all end up/The remains of the day."

They say "it's really okay," but is it? The comedian Woody Allen said, "I'm not afraid of death; I just don't want to be there when it happens." That sort of sums up our situation. We know we will die, and we don't like that.

So, we do all sorts of things to hide from death and all the limitations that remind us of it in various ways. We become obsessed with looking after Number One. We grab for power because if we are powerful, we can make believe death has no power over us. We look for fame and acclaim because we want to believe that we are too important to die. In fact, those were the temptations Jesus faced in the desert. He resisted and went to the Cross.

Throughout history, we have given in to the temptations. We have allowed death to estrange us from God, one another and our own true self. Our refusal to face, accept, and perhaps even in some sense embrace death is the ultimate source of sin.

And so Jesus comes among us to do what we do not do, cannot do. He goes to death with all the fear and disgust that we have. But he goes with confidence in the love of God that is stronger than death.

Because we are aware of death, we can try to avoid it out of fear. But, in the Cross of Jesus, we now know that because we are aware of death, we can face it with hope because by his death and resurrection Jesus has shown us that God's life-giving love does not die. That love is not overcome by death, neither the death of Jesus nor the death of each of us.

And so we mark this Holy Week with solemn joy. Death is real. But this week we know that love is even more real.

Easter Sunday (B)

Construction workers in New York found an Eighteenth Century graveyard for African slaves. One set of bones were those of a six-year-old boy. Scientists found that the lad had been malnourished, diseased, anemic and had broken bones from carrying loads too heavy for his little body.

What was his name? Did anyone weep over his life or death? Did anyone know or care about his pain? When he shivered in the snow or sweltered in the heat, did anyone comfort him? When he whimpered in confusion, loneliness or agony, did someone hug him? The boy lived miserably and died anonymously. What kind of people could inflict such a life and death on a child? Where was humanity?

Where was God?

I need not go back centuries to face that same question. If I look around, how much suffering and loss do I see?

Where is God?

I need not even look beyond myself. I have suffered and will suffer. I will die and even if people weep over that, I will be forgotten, as will those who wept over me.

Where is God?

The good and the bad, the rich and the poor, the wise and the foolish, the beautiful and the ugly — we all go into oblivion.

Where is God?

Easter answers that question. When that boy suffered and died, God was with him. When those I love suffer and die, God is with them. When I suffer and die, God is with me. God is not a spectator. God is a fellow sufferer.

He suffers as we suffer, he weeps as we weep, he despairs as we despair, he dies as we die. He cries out "Where is God?" as we cry out. Jesus' cry on the cross, "My God, my God, why have you abandoned me?" is one with our cries.

That is some comfort. Quite a big comfort, actually. When I have most reason to think that God is lost, that God does not care, that

God does not even exist, then God is most present with me, present with me in the same confused, pained way I am present to myself.

But, Easter says there is more. Christ rose from the dead. His suffering and his death, his confusion and his fear, his doubt and his hope were all embraced by God's love that is stronger than death. His rising from his death is a promise that we, too, will rise from ours.

We do not know what that means. Our statements are poetry more than prediction, and are true as poetry is true, not as almanacs are true. We know that God's love for each of us goes far beyond what we can imagine. Heaven will not fit into our imaginations, into our concepts, into our words.

What can fit into my head and my heart is a conviction. Christ has suffered, has died and has risen. That is the guarantee that we will share his life. He loves me enough to join me in death; he loves me enough to have me join him in life.

And what of that boy in New York or the billions of others who have died, most of them never knowing of Christ?

The place to look for an answer is my own case. On Easter I renew my baptismal commitment. I confirm my belief not only in the resurrection of Christ, but also in my own share in "the resurrection of the body and life everlasting."

Because my death is not apart from Christ's, what happens to me after death is not separate from what followed Christ's death — resurrection. I rejoice and sing "Alleluia!" for Christ and for myself.

And for others. The love of God that is stronger than death knows no limit except, perhaps, our refusal to be embraced by it. All who have suffered have been united with Christ on his cross, whether they have known it or not. God's love will not be cramped by our knowledge or be held off by our ignorance. Those same people, then, are also united in his resurrection.

Our Christian vocation comes from this knowledge. All our brothers and sisters have the right to know the good news that Christ dies and rises for them and with them.

On Easter we celebrate on behalf of all the world God's love that embraces all the world. We celebrate for that boy, for all the dead and for ourselves, the living who are promised a share in the life of Christ who rose.

Second Sunday of Easter (B)

Often when we hear or read familiar passages of Scripture we put a label on them. We hear, "It happened that one of the Twelve, Thomas, was absent." We think, "Oh, yes, Doubting Thomas." Then we stop paying attention because if familiarity doesn't breed contempt, it certainly breeds inattention. Yet, in this Gospel passage, attention to an easily overlooked detail is essential if we are to know what the story has to tell us.

When we wish to emphasize something, we repeat ourselves. Scripture does so, too. Today's repetition is barely noticeable. The passage begins, "On the evening of that first day of the week . . ." That day, of course, is Sunday. The repetition is in slightly different words, but says the same thing: "A week later . . ." The next Sunday. The Evangelist begins each part of the passage emphasizing that whatever is going on has to do with the fact that it is Sunday.

Well, what is going on? For one thing, the disciples are gathered. On the first Sunday, these followers of Jesus come together and the Lord appears among them, greets them, blesses them and empowers them.

But Thomas was not there. We don't know why. All we know is that on that particular Sunday he was not gathered with the rest of the followers of Jesus and so did not meet the Lord. And so, he did not, could not, believe.

The next Sunday, the disciples were again gathered, and this time Thomas was with them. Again, the Lord appeared before them, greeted them and invited Thomas to believe. And Thomas did believe.

The Sunday gathering of the followers of Jesus is the place where the risen Lord approaches us in a special way, offers us peace, blesses us and empowers us. He can, and does, work elsewhere, but this Sunday gathering of his people is a special place for meeting the Lord. Therefore, for twenty centuries we have gathered each Sunday as his followers. It is so important that for Catholics it is an essential part of our life as Christians; we have an obligation to be with the community on Sunday.

Does it always work? Does my being gathered with the followers of Jesus on a Sunday guarantee that I will encounter the risen Lord, that he will say to me, "Peace be with you"?

That certainly has not been the case in all my years of going to Sunday Mass. In fact, more often than not, Sunday Mass is a somewhat neutral experience for me. Sometimes the gathered people, the presiding priest, the music, the church decoration, the weather, my own sinful weakness or whatever can "turn me off."

But, there are Sundays when, like Thomas, I suddenly know the Lord is with me. A prayer, a word of Scripture or the homily, a hymn, the presence of my brothers and sisters, the Eucharist — something puts me in the presence of the Lord or makes me notice him. I go to Mass for those times, and that is where the risk comes in.

Meeting the Lord is a risky business. Legend has it that Thomas's meeting the Lord in that Sunday gathering resulted in eventual martyrdom in India. Others who were in that gathering did not fare better. Often when we meet the Lord in our private prayers, he is a comforter. But I think when we meet him in the Sunday gathering of disciples he more often than not comes to commission us as he did the disciples on those Sundays long ago when he sent them out to confront the sin of the world.

To forgive the sins of the world is to face the sin of the world with the same powerlessness that Jesus had on the Cross. We are sent by him with his powerful weakness to meet the evil of the world with God's love.

Considering that whenever I join my fellow Christians on Sunday, I am putting myself at that kind of risk, going to church must be one of the bravest or most foolhardy things I can do. Who knows where it will lead?

Living a Christian life takes courage. However, we need not search for it. We have it. Each Sunday when we join the community of disciples we take the greatest risk, that of meeting the Lord. If we can, and do, take that risk, the other risks of the Christian life should be easy by comparison.

Third Sunday of Easter (B)

Exuberant joy is the proper way to live the Easter season. Easter is 50 days long precisely because our joy in knowing that Christ is risen and we share his new life cannot be confined to or used up in just one day.

Yet, the joy is paradoxical. In Luke's Gospel, the disciples talking about the Resurrection are terrified when they see that what they are talking about and hoping for is really true. When Jesus appears and gives them a greeting of peace, everyone panics. He has to prove to them he is no ghost by having them touch him and by eating some fish.

What would my reaction be to meeting someone I knew to be dead, someone whose corpse I had seen, someone whose grave I knew? Living in an age more inclined to psychological rather than spiritual explanations, I would probably think I was hallucinating rather than that I was seeing a ghost. Like the disciples, though, I would panic: "Am I cracking up?"

Let's face it — the Resurrection is unbelievable. Even seeing the risen Lord is not going to convince us otherwise. It's easier to believe in ghosts or to doubt one's own sanity. Actually, we don't have to do the doubting ourselves; others do it for us. The wisdom of the world assures us that we're at least deluded and probably crazy in our belief that Jesus, once dead, is now alive.

To understand the joy of this season, we must remind ourselves of the impossibility of what we celebrate. We know as well as the disciples did that Jesus really died. There was, and is, no doubt about it. Even if he had not been tortured to death on a cross 2,000 years ago, he'd be dead by now.

We can be so used to the idea of the Resurrection that we can forget its basis, the death of Jesus. Unless we remember that, we cannot fully celebrate this season. It becomes mere good feelings and folklore.

However, if we remember the fearsome reality of death, we are ready to rejoice over a piece of cooked fish. In the Resurrection, the impossible has happened. A dead man has returned to his friends, spoken with them, shown his fatal wounds to them, eaten with them.

And we are those friends. The best friend I can ever have, because he knows me in every detail, in all my weakness, yet loves me without limit is Jesus Christ. His earlier friends, our forerunners, were "incredulous for sheer joy and wonder." In our own sheer joy and wonder, we remember how impossible it is that our friend is alive after being dead.

He was dead; he is alive. That in itself is cause enough to whistle, whoop and dance. Yet, there is more to our joy.

I will one day die. There is no doubt about it. The one statistic that never changes is the death rate. It is, and always will be, 100 percent. No medical technology, no cloning, no wonder drug, no diet, no exercise, no prayers, nothing will ever change that. One day, I will be as dead as Jesus was. Dead. Done. Full stop.

And yet, through my really dying, I have a promise of new life in Christ's rising from death. United with Christ's death by the Baptism I renewed on Easter Sunday, I am united with his Resurrection. In some way, though I will really die, I will also really live. That's as impossible for me as it was for Jesus. Incredible.

Incredible, but true. Those men and women 2,000 years ago were incredulous in joy and wonder. So can we be. They saw Jesus, spoke with him, were taught by him, ate with him. The impossible, his living again, is real. The impossible, my living again, is real. What else can I do but jauntily, joyfully stride through life?

Well, actually, there is one more thing I can do. The end of today's gospel reading tells us Jesus said that "penance for the remission of sins is to be preached to all the nations." I can be a preacher. Not someone standing on a street corner haranguing the passing crowds, but someone whose jaunty walk through life, whose bewildered joy and wonder proclaim to all who see me the incredible, unbelievable good news that a dead man has eaten some fish. My dead friend is alive. I, like him, will also die. And I too will live.

Fourth Sunday of Easter (B)

I don't know much about sheep, but I have the impression that they are dirty, smelly and stupid. It's no compliment to say someone is a sheep. It implies cowardice, a lack of conviction, a willingness to follow without thought or responsibility. Someone who is sheep-headed is stupid. I don't want to be a sheep.

But I must admit that in many ways I am one. Compared to the splendor of the life to which God calls me and for which I was created, I am dirty, smelly and stupid. I lack the courage and conviction to live as a child of God, imitating the Lord in loving without stint, without fear. I follow where the world leads. Left on my own, I will wander through life, losing my way, following whatever or whoever attracts me at the moment, but never really getting anywhere. I need a shepherd.

What do shepherds do? They protect sheep from their sheepishness. Shepherds ward off dangers that threaten the sheep, who are helpless otherwise. A shepherd also leads sheep from place to place for their own good. Left on their own, sheep might denude a pasture of all its grass and then stand around staring at each other. The shepherd knows where to take them for more food and knows how to force them to move on. Sheep need a shepherd.

Jesus announces himself not merely as a shepherd, but as the Good Shepherd. He is the one shepherd we can trust because he is the one shepherd who is not a sheep himself.

What is the sheep-idity from which he guards us? There are many things in our lives from which we need saving. One of the most dangerous is, perhaps, our tendency to follow false shepherds. We do not usually notice it, because all the other sheep around us are walking in the same direction we are. We go along with the crowd, the flock.

We do not consciously decide to live lives that go counter to our own real best interests, lives that go against what our creator intends them to be. We just go along. We stretch the truth from time to time.

We swallow whole the prejudices against people, races, religions and nations that our society tells us are "normal." We commit many minor mindless insensitivities toward others. We forget God.

It is from all this that the Lord, the Good Shepherd, leads us, but in an interesting way. He saves us from sheep-idity by turning us into shepherds.

In today's second reading, John tells us that in Christ, we have been made children of God. This brings us to the heart of what we celebrate in this Easter season, the immeasurable, incredible love of God. We recall that God's response to humanity's murder of the Son is undeserved forgiveness and more. We kill the Son, and God offers us eternal life, the eternal life of the risen Good Shepherd.

It's hard to believe, because it doesn't always seem to me or others that I am a child of God, that I am one who has received a promise of a new kind of life. John says that the world does not recognize us as children of God. I don't recognize myself as such, either.

John says that in our resurrected life, we will become more like the Lord because we will see him as he is. Jesus says much the same. We know the shepherd, recognize him and follow him. In so doing, we become more and more like the shepherd.

That means we need not be sheep. We can dare to live in freedom. We can take the risk of loving others and God. We can, by the way we live, show others the way God has set for the world. All we need do is keep our eyes on Christ, following him whom we meet in prayer, Scripture, sacrament and the community of his followers.

That is important because a world full of sheep needs real shepherds who by their lives can lead others to the Good Shepherd, Jesus Christ. In our baptism, we have received the vocation to be Christ for the world.

So, perhaps it's not all that bad that I am a sheep. For some reason or other, God has called me to follow the Good Shepherd, who will turn my sheep-idity into discipleship by showing himself to me and reshaping me into a shepherd myself.

Fifth Sunday of Easter (B)

Jesus said, "My Father has been glorified in your bearing much fruit and becoming my disciples." That's not fair. Shouldn't we get the credit for bearing fruit and being disciples?

Though God owes me nothing, part of me wants God to be beholden to me. After all, I try to avoid evil. I even do good. In fact, sometimes I do good or avoid evil precisely because I want some reward from God.

God has given me life and all that comes with it — love, friends, beauty, opportunity and faith. I have already received in abundance. Beyond that, in the Resurrection, God has given me the promise of eternal life. My saying "Yes" to such generosity may be prudent, but it is certainly no credit to me. God should be glorified, not because of what I have done in responding to those gifts, but because of the offer of those gifts in the first place.

The source of the gift is my union with Christ, a union described in the parable of the vine. In Baptism, I am as intimately united with Christ as branches are with the trunk and roots. This is not biological life which I have by virtue of being a breathing human, but the Christian life, a special form of human life.

Today's second reading summarizes Christian life. "We are to believe in the name of (God's) Son, Jesus Christ, and are to love one another as he commanded us." The passage continues, saying that this is the way that we will remain united with Christ, remain part of the vine.

But, what is it to believe, what is it to love? There is really no difference. The word "believe" comes from an old way of saying "be in love." To believe is to love. And love is not just an emotion. True, feelings are part of love, but at its most basic, love is a decision, a decision to act in a certain way toward another, toward others.

That is the reason the second reading starts by calling us to action rather than nice words or good feelings. "Let us love one another in deed and in truth and not merely talk about it."

In the Acts of the Apostles Saul shows what love calls for. He continues to proclaim the fact that he has met the Lord though no one trusts him and some even want to kill him. That is the basic vocation to which all followers of Jesus are called. We must show the world through our confidence in the face of frustration, threat and death that we are united to the true vine, the Risen Lord.

We do this by public proclamation of our faith, uniting in prayer and worship with the community of those who follow Jesus. We do it by unselfish service of our neighbor. We do it by making our faith in Jesus the measure by which we make the day-to-day as well as the major decisions of our lives.

Our objective is to draw others to union with Christ, so that they, too, may share his vocation of showing his Father's love to the world.

We have a tendency to think that living like St. Paul means that we have to be super-human. We feel guilty about not being like him, but at the same time, a bit relieved by the thought that we need not live lives that proclaim the Lord because we are not super-saints.

However, we are too hard on ourselves. God knows us, loves us and calls us just as we are. As John's letter says, we "are at peace before him no matter what our consciences may charge us with; for God is greater than our hearts and all is known to him."

We need not be superior beings in order to live every moment of our lives as Christians. Neither does leading such a life make us into superior beings. When all is said and done, we are merely shoots from the true vine. Whatever we have comes from him, and without him, we are nothing.

That is why God is blessed in whatever we do. It is the work of Christ in us, giving us his life, challenging us with his teaching. So, we move through life, being as faithful as we can, bearing what fruit we can, and rejoicing that God deserves the credit, but has chosen us to be the means by which the divine will is made real for the world.

Sixth Sunday of Easter (B)

One the real saints I've met was a homeless man in Tokyo. He looked like what he was, one of life's casualties. He kept himself in food and drink by collecting scrap cardboard in a cart and selling it.

Every day, he came to a soup kitchen. Most of those who came ate and left. Many would offer thanks for their meal. This man made it a point to visit the volunteers in the kitchen, asking how far they had traveled and thanking them for their generosity. He was a gentleman.

One winter day, he came with a man who had been struck by a car. The center had a free clinic, and the doctor examined him. There was a broken bone in his foot, but the injured man refused to go to a hospital. The doctor agreed that complete rest outside a hospital bed would eventually work as well as rest in such a bed.

From that day on, the gentleman cared for the injured man. The cart became home for him. For six weeks, the gentleman gave his food to the patient. Since the cart was now a hospital bed, the gentleman could not work to earn even his usual poor living.

One cold morning, the injured man shook the gentleman to wake him. He was dead. Six weeks of giving up most of his food and six weeks of sleeping on the winter sidewalk in order that his friend might sleep in the cart had cost him his life.

In John's Gospel, Jesus says, "There is no greater love than this: to lay down one's life for one's friends."

When I learned of the gentleman's death, I was embarrassed. After all, I know these words of Jesus. I know the promise of eternal life. Yet, here was a man who may never have heard of Christ, but who did what I have never had the faith and courage to do.

Gradually, I realized that the gentleman and I had something in common. He was without doubt a saint. That's not what we have in common. What we have in common is imperfection. His problems and imperfections were obvious to anyone who looked. Mine might be better disguised, yet, even so, they are prominent to me, at least.

Isn't it true that we tend to see what is lacking in our lives, in our faith? The broken part of my life overshadows the child of God that I am. From childhood on, people point out our shortcomings. Ask anyone to make a list of his or her failings, and one sheet of paper will not be enough. Ask the same people to list their qualities that show them to be sons and daughters of God, and when the list finally appears after much hemming, hawing and crossing out, it will be short.

Today's continuation of our Easter celebration is a joyous proclamation of the great love God shows in calling us to be united with Christ. It is a day to look at our faults and failings and put them in perspective. Next to God's love, they are nothing. Can I give thanks today for God's love that does not look at my faults, failings and weaknesses?

In the Acts of the Apostles, Peter sees that God's love will not be limited. "I begin to see how true it is that God shows no partiality." God showed love through Cornelius and that gentleman in Tokyo. God can, and does, show that same love through me as well.

"Love, then, consists in this: not that we have loved God, but that God has loved us and has sent the Son as an offering for our sins," says John. All humankind is embraced by that love.

Throughout this week, let's make an effort to see the children of God hidden in our families, our friends, our foes, strangers and even ourselves. Let's look beyond the problems, sins and weakness that too often draw our attention and see how great God's love is.

Chosen to know and proclaim the Son, we Christians are especially blessed. Among our blessings is the knowledge of who it is that acts in men and women such as the Tokyo gentleman. Let us give thanks for that extra love that has called us to know Christ. Let us give thanks for God's love that overflows the Church and shows itself through saints beyond our community, saints we might not even recognize at first glance.

Ascension (B)

The disciples stood around staring upward.

"Hey, Pete, how do you figure he did that?" asked Andrew.

"Beats me. What do you think, Jack?"

John answered, "I dunno. Maybe he used a helicopter."

James sneered, "Don't be stupid. Helicopters won't be invented for almost two thousand years!"

John retorted, "Alright, smartie, *you* say how he did it."

Then, two men in white robes joined them and one of them asked, "Men of Galilee, why do you stand looking up toward heaven?"

Peter pointed up to the sky and answered, "Well, you see, Jesus sort of went up that way and we're wondering how he did it."

"Oh? Did he say anything before he left? Did he tell you to wait here for him? To build a shrine on this spot? To organize meetings or pilgrimages? To go back to your fishing nets?"

"Well, no," Peter replied. "Actually, he told us to proclaim him to the ends of the earth."

Puzzled, the man in white looked at the disciples and repeated, "Men of Galilee, why do you stand looking up toward heaven?"

The Church exists to do one thing. Our vocation is to proclaim in word and deed the gospel of Jesus Christ, God's forgiving and life-giving love. Everything we do — worship, teaching, preaching, work for justice and peace — must be directed toward that. That is the reason the men in white asked the disciples why they were standing around rather than getting a move on.

The way Mass ends is a lesson for us. Once we have heard the Word of God, prayed our thanksgiving and shared the Eucharist, we do not hang around waiting to see what comes next. We are dismissed rather abruptly. "The Mass is ended, get out of here," while not the actual words of the deacon or priest, are the import of the message.

Certainly the Church grew beyond the small group of disciples because Christians did not hesitate to go out and proclaim Christ. They invited others to join them. Peter and Paul did not found the

Church in Rome, they found it. There were already Christians there who welcomed them. Apparently Christian merchants, soldiers, slaves and travellers brought the Good News first and were not hesitant to proclaim it.

Evangelization includes a call to faith in Christ and an invitation to membership in his Church, but is not limited to them. Jesus called some people to follow him, but he showed the forgiving, healing love of God to all. Instead of telling those he forgave and healed that they should follow him, he sent them home to tell others what God had done for them. Every follower of Christ must do as he did. If we do our part, many will not become Christians. Others will be drawn to Christ and join us in our proclamation. Their response is something between them and God.

What, then, is our part? It is right in front of us, if we stop gazing off into space and look around. There are people who are hopeless and confused. There are people trapped in sin. There are people suffering the effects of illness, poverty and injustice. There are people who are ignorant of God's love for them. Evangelization, the fulfilment of our Christian vocation, means finding practical ways to answer those needs.

Seventh Sunday of Easter (B)

Jesus prays for his disciples, including us. In that prayer, there are three characteristics that Jesus seeks in his followers.

The first is unity, "that they may be one, even as we are one." Yet Church history is a story of divisions, heresies, schisms, mutual persecutions, excommunications, hatred, torture and intolerance. The Church of Christ is divided among Catholics, Orthodox, Anglicans and others lumped under the title "Protestants."

Within Churches, things are no better. To hear the way Catholics talk of one another or treat each other based upon differences of spirituality, structure, theology or mission, one would wonder if they follow the same Lord. Can we say that our parishes or families are models of how men and women can come together in spite of differences to build a community that praises God and proclaims his Good News?

Well, what of the second element of Jesus' prayer? "I gave them your word, and the world has hated them for it; they do not belong to the world."

Not only are we Christians very much of the world, but the predominantly Christian part of the world is the leader of the world's economic, military and political power. We are so much of the world that some people even join the Church to have a share in that worldliness. Even in the Church, the values of the world often determine policies and activities. Instead of the world hating us, we and the world get along very well.

Then, there is the third part of the Lord's ideal: "As you have sent me into the world, so I have sent them into the world." We are certainly in the world, but are we there in the same way that Jesus was? Are we a redemptive presence to our brothers and sisters living in fear of death, of sin, of God? We do not usually seem so to most of those outside the Church.

The evidence indicates that either God did not hear the prayer of Jesus or that our selfishness, laziness, fear and sin have prevented the fulfillment of the Lord's hopes. We have blocked the all-powerful God.

We have alleluia-ed our way through the weeks since Easter Sunday. Now, we must temper our rejoicing with repentance and a commitment to live the resurrection throughout the year.

What does that mean? Today's prayer of Jesus makes it clear, if not easy. If we wish to follow him faithfully and be the sort of people he desires, we need only begin to live and act as he prayed.

The first step is to build unity. Unity is not uniformity. It is a recognition of the different gifts and personalities God has given us for the sake of the world. In fact, it goes beyond recognition to rejoicing. We give thanks for our differences, and then strive to support each other's gifts in our common task of showing the world the forgiving, unifying love of God.

Living the second wish of the Lord, being free of the world's values and power, is the really difficult part of Christian life. After all, we depend upon the ways of the world to make a living for ourselves and others. From long experience, we know how to make our way in the world with some degree of comfort, confidence and success. Giving that up is hard. Maybe it's impossible for me.

The way out of our quandary is found in the Lord's third wish, that we go into the world as his heralds, proclaiming him and his message. If we commit ourselves to that, the world will, paradoxically, help us escape slavery to this world.

The reason is that the world itself at its deepest level seeks liberation from the power of sin. People hope that death and futility are not the whole story of their lives. When we go among our brothers and sisters proclaiming Christ's resurrection triumph, they scrutinize us to test our authenticity and the authenticity of our message.

When that happens, we are forced to start living the message we talk about. The expectations of non-believers make us act like the believers we claim to be. What God cannot get us to do, those who perhaps unknowingly seek God achieve.

So, the way to live as Jesus prayed we would live is to start doing it. From the action will come the reality in our hearts, a freedom to walk through this world as citizens of heaven, a unity with all creation that comes from the one God.

Pentecost (B)

The miracle of Pentecost was not that people understood what the disciples said. The miracle was that they said it in the first place. Men and women who had been hiding, fearful that they would be discovered by the authorities who had killed their teacher, suddenly were making "bold proclamations" to people from all over the world.

Pentecost was the Greek name for the Jewish feast that came 50 days after Passover. Though it was originally a harvest festival, by the time of Jesus it was (and still is) a feast celebrating God's covenant with Israel on Mt. Sinai. What happened there is a key to understanding the vocation of the Church that was born on that feast.

It was at Sinai that the people experienced the glorious presence of God. It was on Sinai that Moses received the law of God. It was at Sinai that the mob that had come out of Egypt became a people with a special relationship with God. It was at Sinai that the people accepted that relationship and committed themselves to a special kind of life in faithfulness to it.

The upper room was a latter-day Sinai. At Sinai, the power of God was shown in thunder and lightning. In the room, it was shown in "tongues as of fire." At Sinai, the people were made one by the law of the Lord. In the room, they became one Church by the power of the Spirit. At Sinai, the people learned the laws that would govern their lives and define them as a people. In the room, the disciples were given the vocation that would define the followers of Christ: they became proclaimers of the Good News.

So, the Church was born on the festival of the birth of God's chosen people. But, there was a difference. There was another high place in Scripture that must be kept in mind when looking at Pentecost. That is the Tower of Babel. That tower was built as a way to increase human power; it became the source and symbol of the linguistic and other divisions among people. In the upper room, the legacy of Babel was ended. The disciples spoke and people from around the world understood what they said. The way the world was created, with no divisions among people, was once again present. The new creation was born in the birth of the Church.

At Sinai, God formed a covenant relationship with one people, Israel. At Pentecost, the new covenant was made without borders, without limitations of language, nation or race. The new covenant is for all people. The whole world has become the chosen people.

The Church is Pentecost carried out through history. What happened to the disciples that day happens to us. The vocation they received is the vocation we receive. The bold proclamation they made to all nations is the bold proclamation we make.

That has implications for us today, the anniversary of our vocation to be Church. When the disciples became Church in the power of the Spirit, they did not immediately organize or figure out what to do among and for themselves. Getting the Good News out was more important than what went on inside the room or the community.

The Church exists not to be a club of the saved, but to be the herald of the Gospel. Our first concern must always be with those who are outside, for the men and women who have not yet come to know Christ. Whatever we do as Christians, whether as individuals or as a community, must be shaped by our vocation to tell the whole world the Good News that Christ is risen.

We do not do that as a mob, but as individuals who put our varied and necessary talents at the service of the proclamation. Each of us is essential to the mission of our Church. The gifts I have been given by God are meant to build up the body of Christ so that the world may know him. Seeing us, they should see him. They will see him if we do what he did: show the peace-giving, forgiving love of God.

We never do that perfectly. Our personal and communal fear, weakness and sin always interfere with our attempts. However, the Spirit who made the disciples understandable to people from around the world that Pentecost works through our stumbling, fumbling efforts to get the message across.

Trinity Sunday (B)

Ishmael, the narrator of Herman Melville's 1851 novel *Moby Dick*, describes the harpooner Queequeg unwrapping his god, putting it on the hearth of their room in an inn, praying to it and then putting it away.

Though the number of harpooners has declined since the nineteenth century, there has been no lessening of the tendency to like manageable gods who will do our bidding when we want them, but can be put away when we are not interested or don't want to be bothered by them. They are pocket-sized gods small enough to fit into our ideas, hopes and demands.

Christians say there is only one God. But what we say and how we act do not always match. I have met people who would protest against any suggestion that they are not Christian, but whose attitudes toward Mary and other saints go beyond veneration to idolatry, making them polytheists, worshippers of many gods.

Idolatry is not limited to religious figures like saints. Nations, races and even sports teams are handy pocket gods. Judging from the sacrifices we make for it and our obsessive devotion to it, can anyone deny that one of our pocket-sized gods fits nicely into our wallets?

We even manage to turn the one true God into a pocket god. In every war, God is enlisted as a patron of the armed forces of whichever side happens to be "Christian." When Christian armies fight Christian armies, God is invoked as champion by chaplains on both sides.

In our day-to-day lives, our pocket-sized god is supposed to grant us winning lottery tickets, good weather and a general sense of well-being — the god in our pocket becomes a teddy bear.

More sophisticatedly, we try to fit God into our various philosophies and theologies, cramming God into our brains.

The dogma of the Trinity says "NO!" to all that. Any god that can fit into my pocket, into my mind, into my concepts and into my expectations is too small to be the one true God. Any creation by my desires, hopes, prejudices, selfishness, dreams or intellect is not God, regardless of what I may call it.

Part of the mystery of the Trinity is the assurance that we can learn something about God by looking at beings who have personalities, ourselves. One of the surest things we know about ourselves is that every single one of us is beyond definition, though not beyond relationship. People are not predictable, they cannot be put into our pocket, and whenever we try to capture the essence of another, he or she shatters our neat ideas. I cannot even neatly categorize myself. Yet, we can hear, heed and love one another.

To say "Trinity" is to declare that there is something about God that is, at its core, a relationship of love, love among the Father, the Son and the Holy Spirit. It is a love that overflows to include us and all creation.

From what we know of love among ourselves, we can guess, hope and intuit that the way to come to know God is to love. Love does not squeeze another into our ideas, but allows the other to remain other, just as the other allows me to be me.

It is here that God does for us what we could not do. God climbs into our pockets. The mystery of the Incarnation is that God whom we cannot capture comes into our lives in terms we can grasp. Not in intellectual terms, but in terms of love.

God does not cease to be God. God does not cease to be beyond all we can imagine. However, God shows us that we can be friends, lovers.

Trinity Sunday reminds us that God can "get into our pocket" and become knowable and lovable not because of what I do, but because God chooses to be known and loved, chooses to be in my pocket.

That may be the most wonderful thing that God has done for us. One God in Three Persons is beyond us and would always be beyond us except by a divine decision to be known by us, known as truly other, yet truly loving.

Body and Blood of Christ (B)

We Christians have had some two thousand years to practice following the commands and example of the Lord. And we have had some two thousand years of failure. No one who looks honestly at the history of the Church or its members, at its current state or even at such Christians as (pardon me for saying this) you or me could claim that we have done a good job.

There is one good thing that we have consistently done, however, even though not all Christian communities do it, and not all do it regularly. It is one of the central elements of Catholic Christian life. That is to repeat the actions of Jesus at the Last Supper. We take bread, speak words of blessing over it, break it and share it among ourselves. We also repeat the action of Jesus over the cup and share it. We call it by many names: Eucharist, Holy Communion, the Breaking of the Bread, the Holy Sacrifice, Mass, the Divine Liturgy, the Source and Summit of the Christian Life and so on.

One aspect of the prayer that marks the action is known as *anamnesis*. The word is Greek, as is much of the technical language of the liturgy, since the original language of most of the Church outside of its Palestinian birthplace was Greek. Even in Rome, Latin did not become the language of the Church's worship until some time in the second century.

The word *anamnesis* means remembrance, or more literally, not-forgetting. Not having amnesia. Before we had the New Testament, before we had Church organization or church buildings, we had the simple act of sharing bread and wine to enable us to not forget the Lord and what he had done and said.

Remembering is not simply something that happens in my head. In Scripture, to remember is to place oneself in the original events. For example, at the Passover meal, the Seder, Jews don't talk about what God did for their ancestors more than three thousand years ago. They speak of how those at the table themselves were brought out of Egypt. So, when Jesus told his disciples to "do this in remembrance of

114

me," he was not telling them to learn answers for a quiz. He was telling them to over and over again join him at the table, in his ministry, in his glory.

When we gather to break and share the bread and drink from the cup, we are really present with the Lord and he with us. The presence of Christ in the sacrament is a cure for and a protection against amnesia, against forgetting that the Lord is with us at all times. He calls us, challenges us, empowers us, comforts us and forgives us. The Eucharist helps us not to forget. And, remembering, we can repent, reform and carry out our vocation. That vocation is to be the real presence of Christ for the world even after the liturgy is ended.

When the Mass was translated from Latin to Japanese, the words, "The Body of Christ," used by the minister of the sacrament were translated into a respectful form of the language. After all, the proclamation to which we answer "Amen" is about the presence of God the Son. But, shortly afterwards, the translation was changed to a form that is used when talking about ourselves.

The reason is illustrated in a sermon preached by St. Augustine in 408. "If you want to understand the body of Christ, listen to the apostle [Paul] telling the faithful, *You, though, are the body of Christ and its members.* So if it's you that are the body of Christ and its members, it's the mystery meaning you that has been placed on the Lord's table; what you receive is the mystery that means you. It is to what you are that you reply *Amen*, and by so replying you express your assent. What you hear, you see, is *The body of Christ*, and you answer, *Amen*. So be a member of the body of Christ, in order to make that *Amen* true."

So, on this feast of the Body and Blood of Christ, we once again say "Amen" to being Christ for the world, confident that his real presence with us will help us act as we truly are, his ongoing real presence for the world.

CPSIA information can be obtained
at www.ICGtesting.com
Printed in the USA
BVHW01s2000041217
501838BV00002B/161/P